KU-283-553

Training musicians

A Report to the Calouste Gulbenkian
Foundation on the training of
professional musicians

Calouste Gulbenkian Foundation
UK and Commonwealth Branch
London 1978

© 1978 The Calouste Gulbenkian Foundation
98 Portland Place, London WIN 4ET

Designed and produced by Ruari McLean Associates Ltd, Dollar FK14 7PT

Printed by W. M. Bett Ltd, Tillicoultry

ISBN 0 903319 11 X

Contents

4

Committee of Enquiry into the Training of Musicians

Lord Vaizey	Chairman
Susan Alcock	General Secretary, Incorporated Society of Musicians
Prof. Peter Dickinson	Professor of Music, Keele University
John Hosier	Vice-Chairman, U.K. Council for Music Education
John May	Secretary, Association of British Orchestras
John Manduell	Principal, Royal Northern College of Music
Muriel Nissel	Senior Fellow, Centre for Studies in Social Policy, and formerly Chief Statistician, Central Statistical Office
Anthony Pay	Principal Clarinet, Royal Philharmonic Orchestra
Robert Ponsonby	Controller, Music, BBC
Richard Taylor	Principal, The Purcell School
Marion Thorpe	Pianist, author of music books for children and co-founder of the Leeds International Pianoforte Competition
John Tomlinson	Director of Education, Cheshire
Basil Tschaikov	Member of the Executive Committee of the Musicians' Union and Chairman of the Philharmonia Orchestra
Sir David Willcocks, CBE, MC	Director, Royal College of Music

In Attendance

Eric Thompson, OBE (Observer from the Arts Council of G.B.)

Secretariat
Michael Barnes
Carole Collins
Angela Gendron
Jonathan Masters
Patricia Phillips
Nick Stadlen

Terms of reference

i) to consider the extent to which the trends mentioned in the Gulbenkian Report, *Making Musicians*, have developed since the publication of that Report in 1965, and to consider the relevance of its proposals to the situation in music education that is likely to develop over the next decade.

ii) to elucidate and set down any relevant new facts affecting the training of musicians that have emerged since the publication of *Making Musicians*.

iii) to consider the present provision for education in music in primary and secondary schools in relation to the professional training of musicians.

iv) in particular to consider present provision in music colleges and elsewhere for the training of instrumentalists and singers (whether concert soloists, opera performers or orchestral players), conductors, composers and music teachers.

v) to consider ways of safeguarding and advancing music training at national and local level in the current economic climate and beyond.

vi) to investigate any disparity between the numbers undergoing training and employment opportunities, to consider the standing of the musical profession at the present time, and to review the present arrangements for providing career advice.

vii) to make recommendations.

Chairman's introduction

This Report is one of a series of reports on the arts and training for the arts commissioned in recent years by the United Kingdom and Commonwealth Branch of the Calouste Gulbenkian Foundation, Lisbon. They are 'Going on the Stage' (the report of the Enquiry into professional training for drama, of which I was chairman), then two reports by individuals, Support for the Arts in England and Wales by Lord Redcliffe-Maud and The Arts Britain Ignores (a report on ethnic arts) by Naseem Khan, and finally the reports of two Enquiries that have proceeded concurrently, The National Study of Dance Education, of which Mr Peter Brinson is chairman, and The Enquiry into the Training of Musicians – that is, this one.

This is the second report on music that the Foundation has supported. The first, Making Musicians, by a committee whose chairman was Sir Gilmour Jenkins, was published in 1965. Its main arguments and recommendations are summarised later in this Report. Broadly speaking, while it was welcomed, large parts of its central proposals were never implemented. We suggest in our Report reasons for this; I think they can be boiled down to two – first, that it seemed that the proposals entailed considerable extra public expenditure at a time when the government was going through one of its recurrent financial crises, and, second, that it proposed the reorganisation of the London music colleges in a way that ran counter, not only to their entrenched independence, but to the main thrust of public policy in the field of higher education, with its emphasis on greater development in the regions.

However, by 1973 it became apparent that the position which had led to the setting up of the Gilmour Jenkins Enquiry had not merely not improved; it had deteriorated. There was a feeling that the training of professional musicians had not changed to meet employment needs; and there was a sense of a deeper malaise in some sectors of the profession – a paradox at a time when the reputation of British music has never stood higher. Accordingly the Foundation responded to the request of the profession for a further enquiry and this present Committee was established.

In order to make recommendations we have had to conduct a thorough enquiry into the facts of the present condition of professional music-making and of training for it, and into opinions as to its quality and the need for reform and improvement. Throughout our Enquiry, which has been exhaustive, there has been the most amicable co-operation between us and the musical fraternity. We think that the facts and opinions we have collected are the best available in present circumstances, although there is a need for a far more comprehensive study of training and employment in all the arts. In view of the present economic situation our recommendations are, we believe, soundly based upon hard reality. We have sought to ensure that wherever practicable we should not make recommendations which, if carried out, would substantially increase public expenditure – rather we have sought to make a net saving wherever possible, or a re-allocation of resources to make them more effective. We have also sought to accommodate our recommendations to the realities of existing organisational structures and institutions. There is nothing in the Report which will greatly add to public expenditure or require legislation. It is true that we recommend that realistic salaries should be paid to teachers at the music colleges in London, that extra residential places for music students should be created in London to provide accommodation for most students as in other areas of higher education, and that pupil/teacher ratios should be improved. These do not seem to us to be outrageous requests; nor does the proposal that the specialist music schools should receive more public funds. Off-setting these increases in expenditure, there will be reductions from the fall in music training places at colleges of education. But even so, despite this prudence on our part, should circumstances change, should money flow like water and Parliament turn to music, then perhaps our recommendations might be different as to the letter, but I doubt very much whether they would be different in spirit.

In this introduction I am speaking for myself, and, as a music-lover, I am deeply grateful for the opportunity of meeting so many people who make music and seeing a little of what their professional life is like. To the outsider, like myself, certain major things stand out. First and foremost, music is an art-form that seems to require both intelligence and dedication. Not all professional musicians are intellectually gifted in other directions but a high proportion obviously is. I would go so far as to say that a musical intelligence is as obviously recognisable as, and akin to, a conventional academic intelligence, as any other form of specialised ability. These are vague phrases, deliberately used 'unscientifically', but (like the elephant) a musical intelligence is recognisable and I think it should be so recognised officially.

If I am at all correct, two consequences follow. The first is that the route to musical achievement is often not likely to be too dissimilar to the route taken by others who seek intellectual achievement – specifically, a university degree in music 'makes sense', as it does not necessarily do for dancing or acting – and the second is that it is perfectly legitimate to study music as a general subject (i.e. not just performance) 'for its own sake', without expecting to follow a musical career, but rather to take up a job requiring a trained and critical intelligence. My own major conclusion, therefore, is that music as a general subject is an intellectual discipline in its own right, as well as an artistic discipline, and that there is good reason to suppose that a broadly based musical education, that includes the theory, structure and history of music as well as execution, and above all a degree in music, can be just as much a preparation for – say – a civil service or business career as a degree in history or physics is generally accepted to be. The argument that a general education in music trains the mind, if correct, is important for the future of musical education because it means that a gifted musician does not have to do music 'on the side' if he wants a degree that leads to a non-musical career.

Another major conclusion follows. It is this. The process of musical education and training cannot be dissociated from what might be termed the 'mainstream' of academic education in this country. There are arguments for the special treatment of special subjects which require special conditions for education and training to be effective, but the issue is how far the differences require a completely separate system of institutions from those accepted by the great majority of disciplines. In my judgment, special facilities for the musically gifted are required, and the Education Act, 1976, so recognises, but they are not so peculiar that a special system has to be erected for music. This is an important judgment because if it is correct, then the arguments for the uniqueness of some of the present arrangements are not as strong as they may seem. However, before we get to that stage of the argument which concerns the institutions for musical training, there is a lot of ground to be covered. All of the arrangements suggested depend in the last resort on the volume of musical activity. In dance, for example, the actual volume of dancing, professionally, is sufficiently small for the numbers of participants to be considered as a very small section of the total volume of the activity of the community. That is not true of music. Music absorbs much of the life and energies of hundreds of thousands of people, and the professional life of a considerable number – about 36,000 is our best guess.

Some areas we have only touched on – pop music and jazz, for example – mainly because they are in fact dependent upon the central musical tradition of instrumental teaching and composing. As it is, concentrating on what is popularly known as 'classical' or 'serious' music, we know that the public demand for music broadcasts, for concerts, for tapes and records has grown fairly steadily and shows little if any sign of hesitating. To meet this demand there is a large technical apparatus of recording studios, broadcasters, agents and other people, serving a substantial number of professional musicians.

Alongside the world of the professional musician is a very large amateur music public. For example, there are something like 1000 amateur choirs and orchestras and 1100 operatic societies. These are stiffened by professional performers, who take part in many amateur public performances, and by trained musicians who have never performed professionally, as well as by 'lapsed' professional musicians. Then, underlying this substantial volume of music making and musical enjoyment is a big educational effort. There is some music in all schools; a few primary and most secondary schools employ music specialists; there are a number of specialist music schools and colleges; and there are the university and polytechnic departments of music. Many children learn a little about the theory and practice of music, and the evidence of education authorities and the boards which examine instrumentalists is that about 5%, or nearly 500,000 learn some kind of instrument. Our major axiom must be therefore that we are dealing with a wide variety of people to whom music matters a great deal. It will not escape attention that, while a great deal of this activity is private, ranging from record buying and listening to the radio to playing in amateur string quartets, a substantial part of it involves public money, in subsidising orchestras and opera and in educating and training people in music. It is this public sector that is mainly our concern.

There are two main sorts of musical activity – teaching and performing – which form a musical career. For many professional musicians their work straddles both activities. Probably the greatest number is employed part-time or full-time as class teachers in schools, or as instrumental teachers in schools, colleges and universities. These teachers include some of the best known musicians, both performers and composers, in the country. Though many performers cannot be readily categorised, the performing group divides broadly into those who are singers and those who play instruments, either in orchestras or choruses, in small ensembles, or as soloists. It is the job of musical training to produce both class teachers and instrumental teachers, and all the various different types of performer; and it is very difficult to tell at the outset of training who is going to do what. It follows, then, that there are arguments for training most musicians to teach their instruments, as opposed just 'to teach' and there are arguments for training all potential soloists for orchestral playing, for that is where many of them are likely in fact to find a job.

A performing musician's career is, in some respects, like that of any other professional person – doctor, lawyer or teacher – but it has the added dimension of uncertainty for the most able performers, rather like that of aspirant top flight QCs. It would be impossible to institutionalise the career structure of an outstanding performer; but it would be possible to improve the pay, security and career prospects of the average orchestral player (who is by most standards an outstanding musician); and it would be possible to recognise that for many musicians a period as an orchestral musician – even a lengthy period of a decade or more – may well be a realistic and human career dimension, rather than the 40 years or so uninterrupted pursuit of a single vocation which is the lot of, say, the civil servant. In other words many musicians have a career made up of episodes. This is attractive to the young and to certain kinds of personality. But because it does not fit easily into the accepted conventional mould, it does raise real problems – how do such people get mortgages and pensions, for example – which really matter. In a world where most people have 'steady jobs', the freelance has a hard time, which legislation and administration in recent years have made even more difficult, though there are advantages of course in being 'free'. Of course there can never be any final or fixed solution to these questions, but if more attention was paid to career structure, a great deal of training would fall into place fairly easily, which is not to say of course that its provision would be simple. But at least the objective would be clear. All this has strongly influenced our view as to the proper range and variety of musical training in our society.

Turning directly to training, there are two separate sets of questions. One set concerns the institutions used for training; the other set concerns the kind of training. In reality the two sets of questions are inextricably mixed and it is useful to distinguish them for purposes of analysis. If we look at the places where musicians are trained in Great Britain we see, on the one hand, the universities with (in 1975) some 1700 students in their departments of music. One theory of their place in music is that they train musicologists; but it is self-evident from a casual glance at syllabuses that this is no longer the case, if it ever was. A substantial number of top-level executant musicians come from the universities, either directly or, indirectly, through the colleges of music. It is inconceivable, given the frequent correlation of intellectual and musical ability, that many of the best musicians will not come from the universities; the degrees they confer give access to non-musical and to teaching jobs; the practical musical experience which many of them offer allows people to go into performing; and their intellectual variety is intrinsically attractive to well-educated young people.

Then there is the dwindling group of colleges of education which have trained general teachers with a music speciality, or music teachers with a general teaching qualification. Their ability to teach talented and gifted children affects profoundly the prospects of those who are going to be professional executant musicians. In the near future few colleges of education will continue to exist as monotechnics and the greater part will be found in polytechnics, or institutes of higher education, and it is to them that similar considerations to those that have been raised by the place of music in the universities must be applied. Whereas in 1975 the colleges of education contained nearly 4000 students on general certificate and B.Ed. courses taking music as a main subject, this number will inevitably fall sharply to about 1600 over the next decade and we make proposals for the half dozen or so institutions that we would like to see concentrating on training music teachers for the schools, whether by initial or in-service training.

One of our main concerns has, of course, been the avenue down which most aspirant professional musicians progress, the music colleges. The way in which these colleges are administered varies. Two are privately financed, three receive deficit grants from the DES, one from the Scottish Education Department, and the rest are maintained or grant-aided by local authorities. They contained in 1975 some 4300 students. the eight largest (each with 200 or more students) accounting for about 3200 students. The financing of these colleges, particularly the larger ones, raises a number of issues. The two privately financed and three deficit-financed colleges are all in London. In the long run it would seem that deficit financing is unlikely to survive as an effective means of distributing public money. There are other possible ways of channelling public finance to these colleges and we discuss these later in the Report.

Training class music teachers raises special problems which we discuss at length. The fall in student numbers in the former colleges of education and the prospect of a severely reduced intake of music teachers into the schools is probably the single most important factor in the music training system at the moment. We regard it as fundamental to the proposals we make in our Report. The school population in Great Britain over the age of 5 is due to drop from 10m. in 1976 to 8m. in 1988 and by the early 1980's the teacher training system will be less than one third the size it was in the early 1970's. New teachers will be a drop in the ocean compared with existing teachers and it is therefore to the retraining of existing teachers that efforts must be mainly directed for the rest of this century.

That, then, brings me to the children and young people in the schools. As concerned citizens we obviously want as much good music as possible throughout the school system, and there is evidence of widespread improvement. But our concern here in this Report is with the discovery and nurturing of musical talent among those children from whom the musicians who train to be professional musicians will be drawn. Some things are clear. There are many boys and girls who are 'good at music'. But the potential professional practitioner is perceptibly better than the boy or girl who is 'good at music'. Without going into the vexed question of giftedness, there is an element of dedication which is certainly akin to giftedness, and which certainly needs special facilities. We call the potential professional 'gifted' and among these there is the very small group of 'high-flyers' whom we term 'outstandingly gifted'. (These are purely working definitions for our Report.) The next group down we call the 'talented'. From the first two categories come the vast majority of music students at colleges and universities. In 1975 the intake numbered some 3500, or about 1 in 250 of the age group. It is for those who fall into this musically gifted category that special arrangements need to be made. Some potential professionals will emerge from the wider, musically talented, category for whom a good musical environment is also essential, but our concern is mainly with the musically gifted.

Our recommendations, therefore, must be based on the twin principles of realism and flexibility. We see a spectrum of institutions, most of them producing a mixture of professional players and teachers, and people trained and educated in music who are destined for other walks in life – a spectrum not unlike that of the other major disciplines like languages, mathematics, physics and history. Within these institutions, from our perspective, it is necessary to safeguard the special position of the potential performer and in some institutions his or her concerns must be virtually dominant. There is a diversity of routes to the orchestra pit and the concert platform, and the essential requirement is flexibility in the arrangements that can be made, so as to minimise irreversible and harmful decisions. Above all, we would like to see far more emphasis upon realistic training for orchestral playing. At the age of 21 or 22, talented performers should have the opportunity to emerge fully into the world of actually making music for a living, with specialist and advanced training facilities of the kind that are proposed in this Report readily available to them.

In our judgment this does not require vast new resources; on the contrary; it requires rather, a re-ordering of resources that for the most part already exist. Our proposals are directed, not to a greatly increased total expenditure, but to more effective expenditure, with more money going to a small number of schools and colleges, and savings made by the reduction in the number of students at colleges of education. As far as the training of professional musicians goes, we must again emphasise that the number of students involved is small – even on the broadest definition no more than 10,000, and this includes many reading for music degrees and studying at the erstwhile colleges of education who will not become professional musicians. We think our proposals for improving the facilities and courses in several of the music colleges and for mandatory grants, are perfectly containable within the normal swings of student preferences, and so of numbers, in the higher education system as a whole, without adding to the gross totals of public outlays. We want to make the training of professional musicians more effective and more helpful to musicians themselves and to their audiences. All these matters we discuss in detail in the chapters that follow, as we trace the different paths that the young musician may take through the training cycle. In this introduction I have attempted to set the scene. Our recommendations are set out in detail at the end of our Report.

The Committee held 18 formal meetings, including one in Glasgow and another in Cardiff, as well as a public open meeting at the Wigmore Hall, London. It also met informally on many occasions and, in groups or as individuals, the Committee met and visited many institutions and people. We are deeply grateful for the welcome that we received from the music profession and the help that so many people extended to us, by writing to us, answering our questions and discussing many matters with us. Throughout the progress of the Enquiry the staff of the Foundation, notably Mr Peter Brinson, the Director, have been helpful in every way and we thank them. In particular, I should like to thank

Michael Barnes, our Secretary, for his untiring efforts and his organising and drafting skill. He and his colleagues have been unfailing in their responses to our demands on them. Above all, I should like to thank my colleagues on the Enquiry for the high priority that they have given to our task, which showed itself in the excellent attendance at our meetings and the quality of the individual contributions that they made. Our task has been a formidable one, but we believe it has been very worthwhile.

Vaizey

December 1977

Note:

Some of our recommendations will benefit institutions with which some of us are connected. In particular, Sir David Willcocks and Mr Tschaikov (Royal College of Music), Mr Manduell (Royal Northern College of Music) and Mr Taylor (Purcell School) might be thought to stand to gain from what we recommend and they therefore hereby declare an interest.

Chapter 1
The present state of the music profession

The background to this Enquiry

1. The 1965 report *Making Musicians* concerned itself primarily with an examination of the educational system, in the schools, the music colleges and at advanced level. In the schools it argued the importance of the early identification of talent and its development through an increased number of special music schools at primary and secondary level, leading on to Junior Music School departments at existing colleges, supported by local education authority (LEA) grants, and entry to music college from the age of 16. At college and advanced level the report was in favour of concentrating the education of performers in London, against the prevailing trend at the time to develop new centres of higher education throughout the country, because of the advantages of access to live performance, teachers and future career opportunities for the young instrumentalist. It recommended the amalgamation of the Royal College of Music, Royal Academy of Music and Trinity College of Music into a single national Conservatoire in new purpose-built accommodation fully supported by the Department of Education and Science (DES) in the same manner as the Royal College of Art. Courses would be from 4 to 6 years long and would lead to a Diploma in Performance. Admission requirements would recognise the special nature of musical talent and would be flexible and not require as mandatory the two 'A' levels usually expected for entry into higher education.

2. As a result of the Gilmour Jenkins Report the Inner London Education Authority introduced a specialist music course at Pimlico School, but it is still the only course of its kind in the maintained sector, though five specialist music schools have been established in the private sector, four of them since the 1965 Report. Otherwise the specific recommendations of the Report have not been implemented apart from a modest expansion in the residential accommodation available to three of the London colleges. Perhaps the most important single development since 1965 has been the establishment of the Royal Northern College of Music, following the amalgamation of the Northern School of Music and the

Royal Manchester College of Music, in new buildings in Manchester. The Welsh College of Music is now established in new buildings in Cardiff, the Guildhall School of Music has moved into its new premises in the Barbican, and the Royal Academy of Music has completed the first stage of a substantial building programme. There has also been a significant growth in the number of Saturday Music Centres run by local authorities, youth orchestras, courses at further education colleges for 16-18 year olds, as well as an increase in the number of university music departments, many of them sponsoring chamber groups.

3. But many of the problems highlighted by *Making Musicians* have not been solved and have recurred in the evidence received by us. The funding of music training at college level is still inadequate by comparison with the support given, for example, to the visual arts. Compared with higher education generally, particularly at the universities, resources devoted to training musicians have been small. The poverty of financial provision for music students is illustrated by the London colleges who between them train over 2000 students. In 1975/76 two of the principal colleges were spending less that £1000 per head on their students and, on a net basis, the contribution from public funds was even lower. The average university student on the other hand received an education financed from public funds (excluding board and lodging) costing well over £2000 per head; and with medical students, where staff/student ratios are nearer what is needed for the adequate teaching of music students, costs were over £3000 per head. Amongst the music colleges, only at the Royal Northern College in Manchester, which is housed in new purpose-built premises, does expenditure per head compare with the universities.

4. Other problems related to the training of musicians also still remain. In some fields we still do not produce as many world-class performers as might be expected from a country our size. There is still a need for an extension in the training of those who choose to enter an orchestra, if the standard of the potential orchestral recruit is to improve. The opportunities for a young performer to embark on a professional career are at best haphazard. The present condition of the profession seems to be somewhat of a paradox. Both in London and in the Regions, and in Scotland and Wales, there is a wide choice of concerts and an increasing variety of opera available on almost any night of the year; our contemporary scene is characterised by a richness and diversity of small groups;

we can boast soloists, conductors, orchestras and opera companies of world class, and audiences of increasing size and sophistication. A considerable number of musicians work in the 'free-lance' field. This may involve 'session work' for gramophone recordings (very often backings for pop groups and solo singers), commercial advertising 'jingles', film and television background music, light entertainment programmes and so on.

5. Since 1965 there has also been an increase in the opportunities for musicians to do more than play, perhaps combining performing with teaching as a Musician in Residence at a university, or by giving illustrated talks to schoolchildren as part of a project to reach a greater number of people. Many musicians earn their living by a combination of means and this may well reflect both the diversity of opportunity that the professional musician would like to see available to him, and also an important change in the nature of his attitude towards his career looking forward to a progression through a number of different forms of music-making in a lifetime. Yet despite this outward evidence of well-being this Committee has sensed certain dissatisfactions. Professional musicians, particularly orchestral players, feel they do not have the status and working conditions of their contemporaries abroad and consider themselves poorly paid. Compared with the orchestras, work in the freelance field is often highly paid and many of the finest string players in the country combine session work with some chamber music and solo work. The opportunities in this field attract many of the best players away from the orchestral world and there is even evidence that some of the most talented students from the music colleges are now going directly into this kind of work.

6. The 1970 Arts Council Report on Orchestral Resources in Great Britain highlighted some of these shortcomings. It felt that London's self-managing, non-contract symphony orchestras (the London Philharmonic, London Symphony, Royal Philharmonic and the New Philharmonia) tended to operate an overcrowded schedule of work that permitted very little long-term programme planning which could be specifically aimed at a widening of public taste or the building of future audiences. In consequence this policy has led to concert seasons that, in recent years, are unimaginative and uninspiring; furthermore the maintenance of programmes drawn from a limited and often-repeated repertoire offers little challenge to the orchestral musicians actually playing in them.

7. These orchestras receive their public subsidy through the London Orchestral Concert Board (LOCB) which is financed by its constituent members, the Arts Council of Great Britain and the Greater London Council. As well as contributions to administrative and welfare costs, the Board offers guarantees against loss towards each orchestra's own promotions at the Royal Festival Hall, the Royal Albert Hall, the Fairfield Halls and other suburban concert venues. These offers are related to the number of concerts actually promoted by the orchestras, each of which is required to undertake a minimum number each season. They are reduced proportionately if the promotions fall below the agreed minimum. The guarantees do not cover the total deficit incurred on these promotions which are also financed in part through the profitable recording work and engagements undertaken by each orchestra. This type of work, together with festival appearances, broadcasts and foreign touring, accounts for about two-thirds of their total work schedule during the course of a twelve months period.

8. For Continental symphony orchestras the method and scale of state subsidy differs very considerably and makes comparison with their London counterparts almost impossible. Nevertheless it is a widely accepted fact that the finance offered by the LOCB (relating to only one aspect of each orchestra's work) is dwarfed by the subsidy received by, for instance, the Concertgebouw Orchestra in Amsterdam or the Berlin Philharmonic Orchestra. The consequent tendency to arrange popular programmes reflects, therefore, more a need to balance costs as far as possible rather than the result of a considered artistic policy. Another consequence is that the cost of promoting concerts by these orchestras outside London, where no LOCB and little (if any) local authority subsidy is available, tends to be prohibitive unless the orchestras can minimise their expenses by avoiding long distance travel and overnight stays. By contrast the annual financing of the regional orchestras, which use contracted musicians, enables them not only to service their home town, their region and, occasionally, to tour, but to plan more interesting programmes taken from a wider repertory. The pressure upon rehearsal time is less great than in London, although regional players do not have the same opportunity to supplement their wages with the kind of free lance work that is available to their London colleagues.

The role of the BBC

9. There is no doubt that since the war the most powerful single influ-

ence in British musical life has been the BBC, not only in terms of the public interest it arouses in serious music and the employment for musicians that it provides, but also in the contribution that it makes to the reputation of British music in the world.

10. Nearly all the BBC's serious music is broadcast on Radio 3. This category of output represents a massive investment over many years, having always been one of the BBC's prime commitments as a public service broadcasting system. The BBC's music policy has remained constant, based upon the aims of excellence of performance, enterprise in presentation and variety of content. The repertoire ranges from contemporary work back to the beginnings of Western music. Within this span of time and content, the emphasis goes first on mainstream music, the accepted masterpieces which have hitherto had the greatest appeal to the audience and which, more often than not, are the works which bring appreciation of music for the first time to new listeners including particularly the young. The BBC also accepts a responsibility to broadcast new kinds of music, to make the unfamiliar more familiar and to help develop more catholic tastes: on the one hand to push back the frontiers in time through first class performances of baroque, renaissance and medieval music, and on the other hand to encourage the work of composers of the present day. Thus the BBC has had a part in the process that has extended the regular repertoire back beyond Monteverdi, and at the same time it is one of the main organisations regularly commissioning and performing new works from young composers. The BBC has an obligation to reflect the musical life of the country as a whole, and therefore provides access to its programmes for established orchestras to record in the studio, in addition to its own house orchestras. Mention should also be made of the great contribution by the BBC through broadcasts of music for schools. These programmes form the basis of much of the non-specialist music education in schools and often provide the only source of music education that a large number of children ever receive.

11. The music is produced from various sources: live relays from the concert halls and opera houses of this country, and sometimes from abroad, deferred relays from the same sources, recordings made in the BBC's own studios, recordings from overseas radio stations, gramophone recordings, and of course performances given by the BBC's own orchestras and choirs. Of the BBC's eleven orchestras, accounting for

over 500 musicians under contract, four are symphonic: the BBC Symphony Orchestra (London), the BBC Northern Symphony Orchestra (Manchester), the BBC Scottish Symphony Orchestra (Glasgow) and the BBC Welsh Symphony Orchestra (Cardiff). There has also been the training orchestra, the Academy of the BBC, whose closure we discuss in detail under Advanced Studies. The Promenade Concerts, started in 1895 under Sir Henry Wood, have been organised and financed by the BBC since 1927. All the concerts – generally between 50 and 55 – are broadcast in stereo on Radio 3; many are broadcast in the World Service and some on Radio 4 and BBC TV. During the last seventeen years, the range of programmes has been greatly extended, foreign orchestras have been introduced and numerous new works commissioned. Since 1974 the BBC has also had the responsibility of promoting the Robert Mayer concerts.

12. Although the BBC is subject to very severe financial constraints at present, the fact that it does not have to contend directly with commercial pressures means that it is much better placed than other organisations when it comes to promoting contemporary music. It can do this by direct commissioning and performing, by broadcasting the performances promoted by other organisations, and particularly by the production in the studio of programmes of contemporary music, whether domestic or international. We feel that it is of the greatest importance that the BBC should continue to fulfil this function, and that the country should not take the BBC's contribution to music too much for granted.

Orchestral playing as a career

13. One of the prime movers in urging that this present enquiry be set up was the Association of British Orchestras (ABO). Its concern was that its members were unable to obtain sufficient recruits of the required standard – particularly string players – and the training of those that they did take was, in their view, incomplete. Part of the answer to this problem seems to be not so much that there is a shortage of potential orchestral players, but that some of the best of those who are available do not want to play in an orchestra, because it is a form of music making which does not appeal to them. Although there are often a large number of applications for orchestral vacancies, in some cases these posts have been left unfilled because none of the applicants have been of a high enough standard. In addition, however, there are shortcomings in the life-style and career opportunities available to an orchestral player –

particularly string players – and we feel that if these are identified and remedied, this would go much of the way towards making an orchestral career more attractive to the young musician.

14. Again the paradox arises that we have orchestras of world class and yet there is still criticism of the way we train our musicians and the rewards they receive. Often it seems their skills are acquired as a result of the need to counter adverse conditions rather than as a reflection of good training. For example, the British orchestral player's facility for sight reading is probably in part the result of insufficient rehearsals, which in itself is the result of inadequate finance. Similarly the popularity of British orchestras with international recording companies is to some extent a reflection not only of their excellence, but of their cheapness.

15. The shortcomings of an orchestral player's life can be easily summarised. In the self-managing London orchestras, they include: only token pensions or sick pay, little long term security, playing a limited and often repeated repertoire and the too frequent necessity of working three sessions a day. In the contract orchestras the major problems include the relatively low wages, particularly among rank and file string players who are unlikely to have supplementary means of increasing their incomes through sessions or teaching, the often inadequate performance and rehearsal conditions and the fact that the job entails a good deal of travelling. The willingness of gifted young musicians to consider an orchestral career is increasingly likely to depend on the ability of the orchestras (and the bodies that support them) to offer salaries, conditions of service and security of employment that compare with those available to professionals in other highly regarded fields.

Soloists, keyboard players, composers and conductors

16. Only a few of our most distinguished musicians earn their livelihoods as soloists. They compete equally with the best the rest of the world has to offer, and have only limited protection in this country from competition from foreign artists. It is the best of these who establish the reputation of British musicians internationally. Solo work in this country varies enormously in fees and prestige. Some stars command extremely high fees reflecting their great drawing power, and although this means higher ticket prices, in the case of these stars it often also means full houses and consequently a greater net box office income. On the other hand many soloists often perform for very small

fees. Soloists and freelance players, being individuals and not part of an organisation, may often face difficulties from the way the profession is structured. Because agents for the most part do not manage young artists until they become established, young soloists increasingly have to have practical business experience to cope with their own fees, contracts, publicity, insurance and income tax just like other self-employed people.

17. Pianists have their own particular problems. If their talent is outstanding they may manage to break into the international circuit through auditions, competitions, the right management and some luck, and establish for themselves a solo career. However, if they do not make the top grade there is little middle ground. Unlike string and wind players, there is only a limited repertoire for pianists in chamber groups. Pianists also, of course, become accompanists and teachers, providing the basis for other musical activities such as dance and choral training, opera coaching and repetiteur work.

18. Over the past decade opportunities for composers have been improving. There are more grants available and there is an increasing fashion for first performances, with the BBC and commissioning bodies anxious to discover gifted young composers. However, the exclusively serious composer who does not want to specialise in films or TV or other forms of popular music, is, except for one or two outstanding talents, unable to earn a living by composition without teaching or performing as well. Commission fees, performing rights and publishers' retainers are their basic source of income and the size of fee does not bear enough relation to the amount of time spent on a work. As a result composers are not always able to devote the necessary uninterrupted time to their work. The final result of their work is also affected by the fact that composers do not get sufficient opportunity to hear their work performed. Although more festivals, orchestras, chamber groups and individuals commission first performances, they do not give sufficient opportunity for second and subsequent performances. The Contemporary Music Network run by the Arts Council of Great Britain has in recent years brought a little more modern music to the regions. Some regional arts associations have tried to present composers in their own communities, although this has often been as composers in residence in colleges and universities. But taken as a whole, the opportunities and rewards for composers do not match the quality and variety of the work that is being produced in Britain at the present time.

19. Young conductors, like young composers, are crucially in need of practical experience of performance and in the early stages of their careers they must grasp all opportunities open to them to conduct orchestras, chamber ensembles, choirs, etc. Traditionally, experience in opera houses has been of great benefit in nurturing young conductors in Europe in the last hundred years or so and there is little doubt that there are valuable opportunities to continue this tradition in a limited way in the four national opera companies. Nevertheless it is important to remember that the opera companies when recruiting repetiteurs must look first for keyboard facility and an ability to coach singers rather than conducting potential. If those young musicians who are engaged as repetiteurs are able to capitalize on the wide range of experience they are given at an opera house to launch themselves as conductors, then this is, so to speak, a bonus. It has been suggested to us that the scales of payment for repetiteurs are too closely tied to rates of pay for orchestral musicians, but we do not believe that these arrangements for payment have operated to prevent outstanding young musicians gaining entry to the opera companies. We are told that any vacancy for a repetiteur attracts a large number of well-qualified applicants.

Opera

20. The Gilmour Jenkins Report rightly recognised that an improvement of standards was dependent on increased opportunities for professional performance, and recommended the creation of repertory opera companies in regional centres outside London. Since 1965 there have been very important developments in the number and scale of permanent opera companies. The Welsh National Opera now has its own orchestra and chorus based in Cardiff and is establishing regular seasons in Birmingham. Scottish Opera is firmly established in Glasgow and has recently moved into new premises in the Theatre Royal, while English National Opera (formerly Sadler's Wells Opera and now based at the Coliseum) has expressed its desire to set up an additional base in Leeds. Touring opera has also expanded: Glyndebourne has added a touring organisation to its Festival season and is also providing opera in London at the National Theatre; Kent Opera has become well established; Scottish and Welsh National Opera both now mount regular and enthusiastically received tours; Opera for All continues to tour in England and Wales, and English Music Theatre undertakes periodic short seasons. Moreover, the last ten years have seen a striking number of new operas as well as exciting revivals of neglected works. The result

of all this expansion which has created greater opportunities especially for those embarking on a career, has been a very marked rise in the standards and quality of British singers.

21. This expansion in the opportunities for professional performance has affected the structure of advanced training. The London Opera Centre was established in 1963 to meet the need then for greater opportunities for performance for young professionals. Now the situation has changed and, following the recent Willatt Report to the Arts Council on the present facilities for advanced opera training, the London Opera Centre will be closed and the National Opera Studio is due to be established with greater emphasis on in-company training. But despite these improvements, a number of current problems remain. While increased opportunities have led to an improvement in the standard of singing, this has not always been matched by a corresponding improvement in knowledge of foreign languages or in theatre skills. And more opportunities are needed for students to train specifically to become repetiteurs and conductors in opera companies, a problem we consider in further detail under opera training.

Instrumental and singing teachers

22. Teachers form the largest group of professional musicians, whether as instrumental teachers in schools and colleges, peripatetic teachers attached to local education authorities, teachers in evening and Saturday morning music centres or as private teachers. They have control over our young instrumentalists for a crucial period of their early development. Most instrumental teaching in this country is done on a one-to-one basis and, when students get to an advanced level, they are concerned above all to study with the right teacher. Surveys carried out on behalf of this Enquiry among the members of two orchestras showed that a majority had started with a private teacher while they were still of primary school age. Moreover many players and singers go on to study with a particular distinguished teacher after they complete their college courses and some continue having private lessons from time to time throughout their professional lives. There is even a minority of professional musicians who have never received any training other than from private teachers (sometimes on private scholarships), and the great majority of pianists study privately until they leave school and go to college.

23. But despite the vital contribution of the best instrumental or sing-

ing teachers, it is undoubtedly the case that their remuneration remains low compared with other occupations requiring similar professional expertise. Another problem is the fact that anybody can become a teacher just by offering to give lessons, which means that there is a broad spectrum of ability among instrumental teachers, ranging from the excellent to those without proficient technique or adequate knowledge of the repertoire who can often do positive harm to young talent. The variable quality of instrumental teaching available at local level is often one of the weakest links in the process of training young musicians, and later in the Report we look at ways in which the present system can be altered to improve the situation.

Chapter 2
Training the school-age musician

The way music is organised in schools

24. Before we consider in any detail the opportunities available to the school-age musician, we should clarify some of the terms we use in our description of music in the maintained sector of education. Maintained schools (often erroneously referred to as 'state' schools) include both county schools and voluntary schools. County schools are those schools established, and wholly maintained, by the LEA. A voluntary school is one which is established by a voluntary body, in most cases a church or other charitable foundation. All voluntary schools are maintained (that is to say, their running costs are met) by LEAs: they may not charge fees for admission or for the provision of education. In the case of a voluntary aided school the governors are responsible for providing the site and school buildings, and for keeping the exterior in good repair. Grant of 85% is payable by the DES in respect of the governors' expenditure, and loans may be made by the Department to cover the remaining 15% in respect of the provision of new building and enlargements. Existing legislation permits the promoters of schools wishing to enter the maintained sector to submit schemes for consideration. This facility is available to the governors of schools of music.

25. Since there is no statutory obligation for any maintained school to include music in its curriculum, a healthy musical life in a school depends on two main factors: first, the attitude of an individual school (and in particular its head) towards music; and secondly, the effectiveness of the local authority in supporting the musical activities of a school by supplying it with additional resources, including instrumental teachers and instruments. Qualified teaching staff in England and Wales receive salaries in accordance with the following classifications: scales 1, 2, 3 and 4; senior teacher; deputy head; head. Scale 1 is the basic salary range, and probationary teachers begin at the bottom level of this scale unless they have degrees. Scale 4 is usually the top salary range of teachers who are heads of departments in secondary schools. Most teachers in charge of a secondary music department are on scale 3 or

scale 4. In very rare instances a head of music is in the 'senior teacher' salary range, although in primary schools, many music specialists have gone on to be deputy heads and heads. In primary schools teachers with a responsibility for music are on scale 2 or, occasionally, if the size of school permits, on scale 3.

26. The above scales have been agreed by the Burnham Committee, and are applicable to all qualified teachers in England and Wales; Scotland and Northern Ireland have their own system of classification. A qualified teacher can be a graduate or a non-graduate. To qualify, the graduate takes a recognised post-graduate course in teacher training in a college of education or education department of a university or polytechnic. Non-graduates gain qualified status through a Teachers' Certificate Course, now being phased out. In the case of musicians who have followed a diploma course at a college of music, they can gain qualified status (as long as they have the minimal general educational requirements) by means of a one year course often taken at a college of education. Teachers' Certificate Courses are being replaced largely by B.Ed. degrees, and teaching is fast becoming a graduate profession. It is possible for a specialist in a skill or craft who has no 'qualified status' to enter the teaching profession. This teacher is not eligible for 'qualified' teacher rates, and is paid as an 'instructor'. There is a recommended minimum salary for instructors, but local authorities usually negotiate their own rates for unqualified teachers. These are kept significantly lower than the qualified rates. The teachers' unions are anxious to have a 'qualified' profession as well as a graduate one; and differentials must be seen to be preserved.

27. Within a school the disposal of the responsibility allowances among the teaching staff is determined by the various needs of the school. The number of responsibility points available to a school depends on its size, on the extent for which, for social reasons, the area in which it is situated is regarded as having special priority needs, and on the number of children over a certain age. Subjects have to compete with each other for scale 2, 3 and 4 posts, and for the numbers of teachers in each subject department. Even with secondary schools of a similar size, the number of teachers within the music department will vary from school to school, and so will the responsibility allowances offered to the teachers. In primary schools where there is a shortage of specialist music teachers, there are often difficult decisions to be made about the disposal

of responsibility posts, and music may easily find itself in direct competition with, say, remedial reading.

28. Very few schools appoint full-time teachers to do instrumental work. Instrumental teaching is normally done by visiting teachers, generally called 'peripatetic' by the schools they visit, although there are distinctions to be made between various kinds of visiting teacher, as we shall note in the next section. Visiting teachers usually 'withdraw' children from their timetabled curriculum activities for instrumental lessons. The school music staff is primarily concerned with class music, the direction of choirs, bands and orchestras, and the co-ordination of the work of the visiting instrumental teachers. But a class music teacher who is a good instrumentalist will often teach his instrument in school.

29. The organisation of music within a secondary school will vary from school to school, according to the school's attitude to music. In some schools music is timetabled throughout the school, in others it is timetabled only for the 1st and 2nd years, with later opportunities for examination options. Some schools put an emphasis on group activities and make timetable arrangements so that music can be made in smaller groups than 30 children. Instruments used in schools fall into two main categories: orchestral and band instruments, often on loan to individual children; and classroom instruments (like xylophones and glockenspiels) used for class ensemble purposes. Between them, the local authority and the school (through various funds, including capitation allowance) provide most of the instruments used in school. With enormous demands on its own resources, a school will look to an LEA for help with some of the more expensive instruments.

30. The *Music Adviser* (sometimes known as a Music Organiser or a Music Inspector) advises the local education authority (that is, the education committee of elected representatives, co-opted experts and the chief education officer) on music policy in all places of education maintained or aided by the authority. The Adviser also advises schools on matters concerning music: this includes the appointment of music staff, help for probationary teachers, new approaches to the curriculum, and the provision of instrumental teachers and instruments. The Adviser is responsible for the administration of any budget that is allocated to music. Budgets may cover the building and equipping of music accommodation in new or re-modelled schools; the provision of instrumental

and advisory teachers; and the purchase of instruments lent to schools, music centres, youth orchestras and bands. The Adviser organises the music centres and youth orchestras that are supported by the authority. He or she interviews and auditions candidates for discretionary awards for places at the music colleges and advises parents about their musical children.

31. The Adviser's team usually includes specialist teachers of instruments who may be employed on several different bases. A *Peripatetic Teacher* is strictly speaking a teacher who 'wanders' from school to school. Although all visiting teachers may be described thus, many authorities reserve the term 'peripatetic' for those teachers employed on a permanent basis, forming the nucleus of the instrumental teaching force. These peripatetic teachers, because of their work in schools with groups of children, are recruited as if they were teachers in schools. They are paid the Burnham rates for qualified teachers (if they are qualified) and they receive holiday pay and superannuation benefits like every other teacher. If they are not qualified, they receive 'instructor' rates of pay. A qualified peripatetic instrumental teacher is, of course, eligible to become a class music teacher (and sometimes does).

32. In addition to this team of peripatetic teachers, many authorities employ musicians on an hourly basis to teach instruments in schools. These teachers are usually restricted in the number of hours they can work (often to ten hours), and need not be of qualified status. The local authority negotiates its own hourly rate. But of course the teachers receive none of the benefits (including security) of a salaried post. These teachers are often described as *Visiting Teachers*. They are usually selected by the Music Adviser. A qualified visiting instrumental teacher can be employed by one or more schools for a few hours a week. In these circumstances the teacher may be considered 'temporary terminal' (i.e. contracted on a termly basis at scale 1, set against the allowance of part-time teachers that a school is allocated). In some authorities a part-time qualified instrumental teacher would find it more financially rewarding to take 10 hours a week at the hourly rate, than to teach on a part-time basis for 10 hours at Burnham scale 1.

33. Some authorities operate an 'award' scheme, supervised by the Music Adviser and his staff. Pupils showing some ability on an instrument are auditioned for individual lessons paid for by the authority.

These lessons may be given by peripatetic teachers and visiting teachers in addition to their normal work, and by private teachers. They can be given at school, in music centres or at the teacher's own home. The authority usually pays for these at an hourly rate decided by the authority. Some authorities will extend their award scheme to paying for advanced pupils to receive occasional lessons from distinguished teachers outside the area of the authority, or for paying the fees and expenses of promising pupils to attend the Saturday morning schools run by colleges of music. Most authorities also organise music centres of their own, which operate on Saturdays, or after school, or a half day release from school. These centres often bring together instrumental teachers, both peripatetic and private.

34. *Advisory Teachers* are usually experienced class music teachers (both primary and secondary, but usually the former) who are either seconded to the Adviser's staff from a school, or who are given permanent appointments. Advisory teachers are mostly concerned with in-service training, both in schools and on courses. They help class teachers evolve new approaches to their work, particularly in the face of challenges presented by secondary re-organisation. They also work with the non-specialist primary class teacher who is looking for ways of gaining confidence in handling class music.

The identification of talent

35. About 5% of school children now learn an instrument of one sort or another and, during the 11 years between 1965 and 1976, the number of candidates entered for the examinations of the Associated Board of the Royal Schools of Music rose steadily from 117,000 to 244,000 (see Appendix B for details). There were far more piano players than any other instrument, with the violin coming next, a long way behind. Candidates for the piano examinations increased in number from 72,732 in 1965 to 110,994 in 1976, while violin candidates increased from 9,468 to 26,473. However it is now the case that at the top levels of the Associated Board exams, woodwind instruments are more popular than strings. In 1976, 882 took violin, viola, cello and bass at grade 8, but 1439 took flute, oboe, clarinet and bassoon. Yet, though more and more children are learning to play an instrument (though not necessarily to a high standard) only a small proportion go on to study music seriously after they leave school. In 1976, whereas 9356 passed the grade 6 instrumental or singing examination and 5460 passed grade 8, only some-

thing like 3500 students entered music colleges, degree courses in music and major courses in music at polytechnics and colleges of education. There is thus a disparity between the number of children learning and the number who go on to seek a professional training whether as performers or teachers.

36. It is of course necessary to place these figures in proper perspective. A large number of children who take up an instrument derive great pleasure and educational benefit from, say, playing the oboe but could never hope to get beyond Grade 4 or 5 of the Associated Board or other grade examination. Another large category of children may have enough musical talent to enable them to aim for a performing career, but in fact have ambitions in completely different directions and regard their violin lessons as a passport to an enriched life as a weekend member of an amateur chamber group while pursuing a career as a nurse, an engineer or a lawyer. Thus, even where the system of music teaching left nothing to be desired, one would only expect to see a very small proportion of the children who learn instruments emerging as music students. Nonetheless, it remains a fact that of the relatively few children whose latent musical talent is such that they are potential professional musicians, the number who end up studying music to enter the profession is less than it might be. Whether this is a good or a bad thing, we discuss later; it is clear, however, that music is not regarded widely as a form of higher education that is valid in its own right rather than as a professional training.

37. A key issue as far as the school-age musician is concerned is that his or her talent should be identified correctly at the earliest possible stage. A high proportion of talented children come from families with some sort of musical background and in those cases talent is probably nearly always spotted when it exists. But talented children born into families with no particular music or cultural background often depend on class teachers, head teachers and music advisers to seek them out. The Royal Northern College of Music provided the Enquiry with an analysis of the social class background of the fathers of the student intake for the three years 1974 to 1976 and this showed that over 60% were in administrative, managerial, professional or technical occupations. This proportion is even higher than for university students and it illustrates the extent to which having the right parents still governs future careers in the music profession.

38. If he or she is to stand a chance of becoming a professional violinist or pianist, the young musician should start to play seriously by the age of 7 or 8, and wind or brass players cannot normally afford to leave it much later than about 11. The identification of talent is therefore of great importance at the primary school. But in primary schools especially, the role of the class music teacher goes far beyond the identification of talent. The class music teacher must be intimately concerned in the whole process of 'sparking off' latent musical talent, as we see when we examine training during the early years (5-11) in the next section.

39. It is particularly important while discussing the process of identifying and sparking off musical talent to say a few words about the scale of the problem. In absolute terms the number of children whose talent is such that they are potentially of professional musician calibre is very small. We have already noted that about 3500 students each year have been entering music departments in colleges and universities. In geographical terms this is about seven a year in a town the size of Oxford or about fourteen a year in a London borough. Assuming they can be identified at the age of 8, this gives a minimum total of about 30,000 school children out of a total school population in Great Britain in 1975 of 10 million. This is the number who, given no change in present circumstances, would be likely to follow a musical training. Clearly the number of musically gifted and talented children is much larger and, as far as potential professional musicians are concerned, it is essential to start with a broad group within which they can be more readily identified.

40. Paradoxically, however, the small number of children involved gives a misleading impression of the size of the problem facing those whose concern it is to ensure that the nation's reservoir of talent is identified and developed to the full. For it is precisely in those circumstances where parental encouragement, expert tuition and professional guidance are least available that the greatest wastage of talent is likely to occur. The alertness of a class teacher, the interest of a head teacher, the priority given to the music adviser's budget by the local authority may make all the difference between a career as an orchestral performer and a life spent without even realising, let alone developing, a major artistic talent.

41. All musicians with experience of auditioning children agree that it

is much easier to assess attainment rather than potential. But they also agree that the outstandingly gifted child is immediately recognisable and unmistakable, and very rare. A child's performance in many traditional musical tests often relies on previous experience of similar tests, and the vocabulary to express the answers. The Chetham School of Music have developed a method of testing which sets out to reveal children's musical resourcefulness and creative responses, and is flexible enough to be adapted to suit the experience and personality of individual children. Common to musically gifted children are such things as an acute ear and an unwavering sense of pitch, an instinctive musical understanding, a concern for the sheer quality of sound, a lively sense of rhythm and a good memory for tunes, kinetic skill, motor-visual co-ordination and an ability to handle classroom instruments or a recorder in a way that seems 'professional' or to the manner born, and, perhaps most important of all, motivation. These are the pointers that can help the non-specialist class teacher to spot a musically gifted or talented child.

42. **We stress, therefore, that the need to pay more attention than has hitherto been the case to the identification of musical talent applies in equal measure to all schools and local authorities throughout the country. LEA music advisers should draw up guidelines that will help to alert primary school heads and their staff to what may be real musical talent in a child. It should be borne in mind that musically gifted children need special facilities and support at a much earlier age than is the case for any other subject, except possibly dance. Opposition to such provision on the grounds of 'elitism' is, in our view, wholly misguided. On the wider question of the nature of giftedness and talent and how to deal with it, we believe that there is much to be learnt from experience in other areas – not just in the arts or languages or the sciences but also, because performing skill is closely associated with physical development, in non-academic areas such as sport. The skills involved may be different, but the nature of the gift itself – and its importance to the possessor – are similar.**

The school-age musician: the early years, 5-11

43. Primary schools are on the whole small schools. The average size is just over 200 pupils between the ages of 5 and 11. As we have seen, there are several salary ranges for teachers, related to their responsibili-

ties. In general, in small schools only the head teacher and the deputy are on the higher scales. This means that it is rare for a music specialist to rise to a more highly paid post (for example 'scale 3' in the jargon) in a primary school and it is likely to become even rarer with falling rolls and thus smaller schools. What is more usual is for music to be in the hands of a teacher who may be a music specialist, but who is primarily a class teacher who, in addition, takes music throughout the school. But that still leaves many primary schools without a music specialist and indeed a few without anyone on the staff who can even play the piano. For example, in about 800 primary schools for which the Inner London Education Authority (ILEA) is responsible, there are approximately 300 teachers with scale posts for music, but only about 10% of these are on scale 3.

44. Very few students we met during the course of our discussions attributed their development as performers to anything that happened to them in class music in primary school. In the report (1976) of the Schools Council working party enquiry into the education of musically gifted children, reference was made to some interviews with students at two music colleges, and to the questionnaires that these same students completed. From that particular sample only two students acknowledge any musical debt to their primary schools. In one case, recorder playing provided a direct line of development to a wind instrument. In the other, the headmistress gave the child piano lessons. On the other hand thousands of young players take up an instrument through the auspices of their school and local education authorities, but this has little to do with class music.

45. In order to bring the problems into sharper focus we decided to compare the music teaching in various schools. At one end of the scale we identified a county primary school with a strong music tradition. The school has 350 children on the roll. The music specialist on the staff is responsible for the co-ordination of the teaching programme and is assisted by 3 peripatetic music specialists employed by the Authority, as follows:

1 peripatetic teacher (violin and 'cello) – 1 afternoon per week
1 peripatetic teacher (clarinet and flute) – 1 day per week (i.e. ½ day for each instrument)
1 peripatetic teacher (trumpet, cornet, trombone, euphonium) – 1 afternoon per week

Initially the music specialist had taught all the above instruments herself; the injection by the Authority of additional specialist assistance in the form of peripatetic staff has now relieved the teacher of the instrumental teaching. The peripatetic teachers therefore undertake the teaching of their respective instruments. There is of course close co-operation between the full-time music specialist and the peripatetic staff. If a pupil wishes to take Associated Board examinations, the peripatetic teacher involved undertakes this work, supervising practice etc. Peripatetic staff also supervise the practice of music prepared by the full-time teacher for concerts. The instrumental teaching programme is therefore a co-operative venture with the full-time teacher acting as the focal point. The music specialist gives additional help to those children who require it. There is a practice room available in the school and pupils have ample opportunity to practise at various times throughout the school day and after school. Two orchestras have been formed to cater for the growing number of children now playing instruments and for the varying levels of ability. Each orchestra comes together for an hour each week. The music played will have been practised previously both individually in appropriate group sessions supervised by the peripatetic staff. The orchestras play together for pleasure and also to rehearse programmes for forthcoming concerts. Smaller groups (strings, brass, woodwind, tuned percussion) also come together regularly. Instrumentalists are used regularly in class music lessons throughout the school, undertaken by the music specialist. Instruments taught at the school are:

Violin	Trumpet	Recorders (descant, treble, tenor)
'Cello	Cornet	Guitars
Clarinet	Trombone	Percussion
Flute	Euphonium	

46. A primary school in north London presents a striking contrast. It is bounded by an extremely busy main road. The area is heavily built up and accommodation is almost entirely terraced houses providing homes for three or more families. The area is highly multi-racial and many of the children experience serious social and emotional problems. A highly talented music teacher left the school in 1972. This member of staff had taken music throughout the school. Both the formal musical activities and the creative music was of a very high standard and the school was used by a former music inspector for demonstration work. On the music specialist's promotion to a deputy headship elsewhere, the

school's music declined rapidly. Nobody on the staff was able to take over musical activities. Although the head has been looking for a part-time music teacher (without success) he now finds in the present economic situation he does not have the finances to support such a teacher, even if he were to find one. One member of staff has some musical ability, at the level of playing a few guitar chords and singing with her own class. Another member of staff takes about 40 children for recorders. These groups take place in lunch-time or after school as does the school choir. A new member of staff joined the school in September who is willing to take some class singing. Nevertheless only 45%-50% of the children in this social priority area school will be receiving any kind of musical experience in their primary school.

47. Since *Making Musicians* appeared, creative music activities have become more prevalent in primary schools. The DES report in *Education* (No. 63 of 1970) on creative music in schools gave cautious support to these activities, and saw them in the context of the child's general, as well as musical, development. Many non-specialist teachers use these creative approaches, beginning with the exploration of sound, and the organisation of sound materials into simple structures through discussion and group work, as educationalists rather than musicians. They believe this is the contribution to a child's education through music that they, as non-musicians, can most effectively make.

48. But some of those who gave evidence to us have seen creative music-making as a barrier to the acquisition of more traditional music skills, such as accuracy of pitch and rhythm in singing and the ability to use musical notation. Indeed, one of the disturbing trends which was drawn to our attention is the decline in disciplined class singing, which can often provide a solid basis for awakening young children's interest in music as well as providing a context in which even the non-music specialist class teacher can begin to identify the early stirrings of young talent. The problem is to find the right repertoire that children find relevant and worthwhile. **We believe that BBC schools broadcasts have an important role to play here, and that their encouragement of class singing (as well as their introduction of other appropriate musical activities) is of great benefit to primary schools.**

49. The ideas of Kodaly, Orff, Suzuki and Rolland can also be very important in developing musicianship to a high level at an early age.

A note on the evidence we received about these methods is contained in Appendix C.

50. The Schools Council project 'Music Education of Young Children' is sponsoring multi-media kits to help children acquire a knowledge of notation, by working through the materials individually and in small groups. The kits, currently being published commercially, are designed for the primary school teacher with little or no knowledge of music. How far these kits can be valuable without a stimulating musical environment to back them up, or how far both children and teachers can handle the musical materials without the support and expertise of a confident musician is at this stage difficult to say. Some specialists have embarked on teaching their colleagues the basic techniques of guitar and recorder playing after school and we welcome this.

51. **We recommend that music specialists in primary schools and music advisory teachers should be encouraged to pass on their skills to non-specialist teachers. The non-musician general primary class teacher is prepared to tackle most subjects except music, which has acquired such a mystique that teachers feel afraid to touch it. But the music specialist and advisory teacher can show the general class teacher how to handle certain musical activities with children that would be within the competence of most of them without musical training. This should include the proper use of broadcasts. In particular, promotion prospects in primary school music should be better, with more provision made for posts on higher salary scales (grade 3, in Burnham Report terms, is what we have in mind, where the schools are of an adequate size).**

52. Most authorities use peripatetic teachers, who may be full or part-time, to give individual or class music lessons in schools. It is worth underlining here the importance of integrating peripatetic instrumental teachers more closely into the fabric of school life. It is too often the case that a peripatetic teacher has no contact with the class, or indeed any other teacher of a child to whom he is giving piano or violin lessons, with the result that the child's instrumental teaching is completely divorced from the rest of his education. Just as it must be of some help to the piano teacher to have some idea of the pupil's general background and educational progress, so the school should not be altogether in the

dark about what is an important area of his life. A peripatetic specialist may have a lot to tell a class teacher about the pupils she teaches. **To this end, several primary schools have adopted the practice of nominating one class teacher to be responsible for liaison with visiting instrumental teachers and we recommend that this practice be developed more widely.**

53. All the evidence we have received reaffirms that violin, 'cello and piano tuition must start when children are as young as possible. The young pianist particularly has considerable difficulties. LEAs have done very little to organise piano tuition as they have with orchestral instruments. For the most part, piano teaching is in the hands of the private piano teacher; and these teachers can be of varying quality. Very few authorities offer free piano lessons to beginning pupils; and the facilities that schools can offer for practice are extremely limited, yet more children seem to learn the piano than any other instrument. To become a pianist means to come from a family that can afford a piano, in a home where a piano can be tolerated and accommodated.

54. All the evidence also reaffirms that early instrumental teaching must be of the highest possible calibre. There have been many comments on the quantity of children learning string instruments and the overall poor quality of their achievement. Instrumental and general musical tuition for gifted children of primary school age may happen in several ways – through a good private teacher, who sometimes organises ensemble work with talented pupils; through an LEA peripatetic or visiting instrumental teacher; through an LEA Music Centre where the best local 'private' teachers and peripatetics teach talented children on Saturdays, after school or (in the case of the new Tower Hamlets string teaching centre) a half-day release during the week; through the Saturday morning Junior Exhibitioner scheme of the Colleges of Music; or through day attendance, or more probably, boarding at one of the specialist music schools (at present about half the LEAs are maintaining, or are prepared to maintain, children of outstanding musical talent at these schools). The choice before a family clearly depends on geography, parental income, LEA generosity and the personality of the child.

55. **In our view it is inescapable that at this age the bulk of the provision for teaching the musically gifted and talented will be in centres outside the primary school. Where a gifted or talented**

child has been identified, we believe that local authorities should be prepared to subsidise private lessons more widely than they do now. In particular, we recommend that one way of meeting this problem would be for LEAs to draw up panels of local instrumental teachers whom they consider suitable to teach in Saturday and evening music centres and to give private lessons to pupils sponsored by the LEA out of school hours.

The school-age musician: 11-18

56. Three years after the publication of *Making Musicians* the Schools Council published the results of an investigation into the views of a large cross-section of early school leavers about what they had studied at school (Enquiry I, 1968). Two tables were drawn up for the subjects normally found in the secondary school curriculum, putting them in order of popularity for 'interest' and for 'usefulness'. Music came bottom of both tables, showing itself to be less popular, by a substantial margin, than religious education or foreign languages, both subjects traditionally found to attract little enthusiasm amongst secondary school pupils. This report stimulated some soul-searching amongst musicians and educationalists. Why was music failing so abjectly as a class subject? Was it badly taught? Or was it *what* was taught that was wrong? Were the musical experiences and facts that teachers (themselves trained in the tradition of classical music of the concert hall, church and opera house) taught, totally unrelated to what children wanted and needed from music?

57. If nothing else, the report helped to confirm the gap between the musical interests of the majority of children at secondary school and the musical culture that is the concern of this Report. The attitude of the majority of children to so-called 'classical' music presents enormous problems to class music teachers anxious to develop a taste for serious music, which may only be of interest to a minority of the children they have to teach. New approaches have been developed in class to involve children in all kinds of music and music-making, including pop, rock and the avant garde, but we ought to sound the warning that this changing attitude to music, and especially 'classical' music, in secondary schools may account in part for the shortage of good young string players coming forward for professional training.

58. The problem for music teachers in the secondary school is that they

have to be concerned with many kinds of music. The extra-curricular activities, the bands, ensembles, orchestras and choirs see them in the traditional roles of performer and conductor, but often with a whole new kind of repertoire to learn. In class work they have to lift music from the bottom of the league. The current Schools Council Secondary Music Project is primarily concerned with the role of music in education, rather than the training of musical talent. It has been looking at and disseminating ways and materials that teachers have introduced to make classes and groups of children sensitive to sounds and to use sounds in a creative way by 'exploring their emotional and sound potential'. These approaches are intended for all children, not just the so-called musical ones, or those with instrumental ability. As no traditional expertise or technique is expected, the sounds tend to belong to the world of contemporary music and to be concerned with colour, texture and dynamics. This has disturbed many traditionalists in school music. Yet traditional approaches in the secondary classroom have not been markedly successful.

59. The typical secondary school has been growing larger, though as the school-age population is now falling, the average size may once more fall. The majority of secondary schools have a music specialist. Their pupils also make use of music centres, and provide the members of the county or borough youth orchestras. An indication of the scale of music provision in secondary schools at the present time can be seen from the following example of a comprehensive school with 1500 pupils.

60. The school is a 12-form entry comprehensive school. The music specialist staff consists of the head of department and two half-time assistant teachers, supplemented by 2 peripatetic specialist teachers. All pupils in the first two years take music, which is approached in a wholly practical manner with pupils allowed to choose from a series of options; class music, percussion, woodwind, piano, brass, strings, guitar, singing. The year group (approximately 350) is broken down so that one third has music whilst the remaining two thirds have P.E. or games. The system operates over three days each week so that all pupils have one hour's music tuition per week. At the beginning of the first year each pupil is required to choose from the options available, listing in order of preference those he or she would like to follow. Each option is followed for one term and every pupil must at some stage in the two

year period follow for one term one of the performing options (i.e. singing or class music). Every pupil will follow his/her first preference at some stage (usually the first term). The option groups also ensure smaller groups (between 15 and 20 pupils in some). The head of department is responsible for the organisation of the teaching programme but the success of the scheme depends on the staff involved. The peripatetic staff are much involved, teaching various instruments within the option groups and regard themselves as part of the teaching staff establishment of the school. The number of pupils in the first and second years learning various instruments, and the teaching staff involved, are as follows:

Percussion	62	(peripatetic staff)
Brass	62	(trumpet, cornet, tenor horn, trombone – peripatetic staff)
Strings	54	(violin, viola, cello – peripatetic staff)
Woodwind	138	(recorder, flute, oboe, clarinet, saxophone – head of department)
Piano	79	(assistant teacher)

There is a good deal of interplay between these option groups with all staff involved in the teaching of all instruments, in addition to their specialism. The accommodation within the school for music is good with several rooms for practice. All teaching staff involved supervise practice at lunchtimes and there is a time-tabled arrangement for supervised extra practice for the various instruments after school during the week. The school has also bought its own instruments which pupils are allowed to take home to practise – these are returned daily for music lessons for other pupils. If a pupil decides to specialise he will then buy his own instrument, if he of she and the parents so wish. There are flourishing guitar groups and a school band has been established which meets after school. The band rehearses regularly and gives concerts for parents, and others. The school also has a choir. In the third year pupils are allowed to choose whether or not to continue taking music. For those who do so, the course is equally divided between work on a chosen special study and chosen instrumental work. In the fourth year pupils may opt again for either a CSE or GCE 'O' Level course.

61. We wonder how far the training of musicians for teaching has taken account of the reality of the contemporary secondary school and the changing structure of education. We investigated the school back-

ground of the students of three of the London music colleges and also of the Royal Northern College and the Birmingham School of Music and found a very consistent proportion of about one half coming from independent and direct grant or maintained grammar schools. Most of the maintained – and some of the direct grant – schools have now been merged into the comprehensive structure and the change offers a challenge to music teaching in secondary schools. The skill of the performer and conductor are only part of what the modern teacher needs, as is a knowledge of harmony, counterpoint and history for GCE work. Teachers often also work at conducted improvisations, supervise and stimulate creative class activities, arrange music for class ensemble instruments, teach the synthesiser, suggest pop projects for CSE and so on. Only those institutions that are very much in touch with schools, and who have staff available with experience of teaching in them, can really offer the kind of training – initial and in-service – that a modern teacher needs. We deal with this in our chapter on teacher training.

62. For the gifted young musician seeking a professional training, important decisions have to be taken at the age of about 11. Perhaps the first prerequisite of an adequate response to the challenge of providing specialist music education is a realisation that all the familiar arguments about elitism and unfair preferential treatment that dominate so much of the national education debate are quite out of place in this context. The Education Act 1976 specifically recognises music as an exceptional case and one to which the educational, social and political arguments against selection do not apply. The number of musically gifted, or even talented, children in any area is statistically insignificant. Their educational and technical requirements are highly specialised and the amounts of money needed to meet them are miniscule. **LEAs should, therefore, be prepared to provide musical training in whichever of the ways outlined below is most appropriate to the particular circumstances of an individual area and the particular needs of each individual pupil.** As will be seen, the options may range from paying for fees at a specialist school or for piano lessons with a local private teacher, to organising a system of peripatetic instrumental teachers, setting up music centres or even setting up a specialist music wing in a local comprehensive or a sixth form college. All of these schemes are in operation in different parts of the country and it is impossible (and indeed unnecessary) to say that any one is better than the others. Each LEA should take the initiative in providing for the needs of its own

children, and should be flexible in the policy it decides to adopt. The options are as follows:

Specialist music schools

63. One obvious solution for LEAs is to use specialist music schools, but important questions immediately arise. For example, does putting children in special schools reserved for gifted musicians help or hinder the development of their personalities? Moreover, many parents of junior age children may not wish to have them living away from home. Parents, teachers, and music advisers will have to weigh very carefully all the factors involved before committing a musically gifted child to one course of study rather than another. However, in some cases there may be overriding practical arguments in favour of sending a child to one of the specialist music schools. A local authority may not be able to provide for its gifted young musicians for several reasons: it may not be able to bring children who are geographically remote to a music centre; it may not have a music centre; it may have no appropriate instrumental teachers; and above all it may have no means of providing for daily musical training, practice and experience. **We would urge such authorities to support their gifted children at specialist music schools. The financial commitment will be slight as such children are rare.**

64. We review the existing specialist schools later in this chapter. All we would say here is to reiterate our plea to LEAs not to rule them out, *a priori*, for political reasons or out of misguided local chauvinism which is offended at the idea of a particular borough or county losing a star pupil. Local pride, however well meaning, must give way to the individual needs of the child who may be a potential professional musician.

The Pimlico Experiment – specialist music wing in a comprehensive school

65. *Making Musicians* recommended that 'Local Education Authorities should make more provision for special schools with music as a major subject, both at primary and secondary levels'. As a direct result of this recommendation, the Inner London Education Authority (ILEA) incorporated a specially music-biased course into one of its new comprehensive schools, Pimlico, in 1971. Each year, primary school children from the whole Authority, with outstanding instrumental ability or potential, are invited to apply for the 15 places available annually in

this 10-form entry school. The children are part of the normal secondary intake and take most of their lessons in classes with their peers. They do have, however, specially time-tabled music activities which include individual tuition in two instruments, ensemble groups and general musicianship. Their first study is normally an orchestral instrument and the second normally the piano. There are a number of before-and-after-school activities including aural classes, orchestra, choral groups, and so on. The young musicians on the special course have the advantage of working alongside the cross-section of children found in an ordinary comprehensive school. They are not protected or cut off from the ordinary world of non-specialist musicians. There is also the advantage that if a child loses his commitment to music, he can drop the special musical activities and remain in the same school. Conversely, a child in the main school who develops his or her musical talent can move into the music-biased group. The demands of the music course naturally make for complex time-tabling problems to preserve as many options as possible for the musicians. The course also needs special accommodation for tuition, practice and ensemble work. The staffing implications require specially sympathetic consideration from the local authority, and peripatetic staff help out the regular instrumental teachers.

66. The attention of the DES and LEAs should be drawn to problems of running a course like this in a maintained school without additional Burnham responsibility points. A special course cannot run at the expense of the rest of the school; and although the children on the course are numbered with the rest of the school, their activities must be considered as an extension to the normal school. There is, at Pimlico, a Head of School Music as well as a Director of Music who directs the activities of the 100 or so pupils on the music course. There is encouraging interaction between the music staff who all teach main school classes as well as the specialist groups. Children from the main school also play instruments and join the choirs and orchestras. In fact, many children are attracted to the school by the musical opportunities it offers. The work load in the music course must be carefully supervised, particularly as the children tend to be of rather above average ability and may be tempted to take too many 'O' levels, to the disadvantage of their music. But at 11 it is not always possible to forecast which children will ultimately wish to become professional musicians, and parents naturally want other career opportunities to be open for their children,

should a musical one prove impracticable. About half of the first 15 specialist musicians (1971 intake) are now seriously preparing themselves for a musical career, but all of them will clearly continue making music all their lives.

67. Much has been learned from the Pimlico experiment which could be of benefit to other authorities thinking of setting up a similar project. In particular it has demonstrated that it is unrealistic to assume that a specialist music wing catering for about 100 children can be grafted onto a normal comprehensive school without making available an extra quota of teachers and accommodation. **Having said that, we feel there are other parts of the country, notably in the larger conurbations, where the Pimlico model could make a valuable contribution to the provision of specialist music education, without duplicating the role of the existing specialist music schools.** Half the population of Great Britain lives in or near the eight metropolitan authorities – Greater London, Greater Manchester, Merseyside, South Yorkshire, Strathclyde, Tyne and Wear, the West Midlands, and West Yorkshire – while over four-fifths of the population lives in or near towns of over 100,000 people, including large cities like Bristol, Leicester, Nottingham and Southampton. It follows that in many of these places a specialist music department attached to a comprehensive would certainly have enough pupils to be viable and could be sufficiently near for a daily journey (albeit a long one). Naturally this will not be a practicable solution in remoter areas, though we were interested to learn, when we visited Scotland, of the proposal of the Working Group under the chairmanship of Mr A. B. Cameron that a specialist unit with hostel accommodation attached should be set up in a secondary school in Glasgow or Edinburgh to provide specialised education for gifted young musicians and dancers. This proposal is being considered by the Convention of Local Authorities in Scotland.

Children in ordinary schools: peripatetic teachers, private lessons, music centres, youth orchestras and junior departments of music colleges
68. For the foreseeable future the majority of musically talented children are likely to attend ordinary secondary schools without any specialist music bias and their musical development will be largely dependent on the quality of instrumental teaching available either in school, at local music centres or with private teachers.

69. This is one of the areas in which there is scope for improvement. Time and again in the course of our enquiries, witnesses complained to us about unacceptably low standards of instrumental teaching. London in particular and the other major centres of musical activity are full of experienced orchestral players and potential soloists who would be only too pleased to spend a few hours each week giving piano or violin lessons, either in schools or at home. We must observe, however, that such service is likely to be hard to time-table, and we suggest that it is best given after school hours, or on Saturday, at music centres. Local authorities usually require certain minimum teaching qualifications before someone is allowed to teach more than a specified number of hours in school premises and in school time. As has already been pointed out, the majority of musicians who seek careers as professional performers have done their training in music colleges without either taking the music teacher's diploma or going on to a college of education afterwards. **These musicians represent an invaluable reservoir of experience and technical accomplishment which we believe it is important to tap to the fullest extent possible.**

70. Some professional instrumental players teach in the music centres that have proliferated since the 1960's and some are registered with an LEA as peripatetic teachers, but this varies from authority to authority and there are some LEAs whose system of peripatetic teachers is barely more than a gesture. The rest teach, if they teach at all, privately. The problem here is that a large number of authorities either neglect or refuse to subsidise private instrumental lessons, either directly or indirectly, in the form of awards to pupils. We cannot emphasise strongly enough that private teachers account for a large proportion of all instrumental teaching in this country and it is probably no exaggeration to say that piano teaching would virtually come to a stop without them. There are many places where, due to the lack of music centres or schools with adequate music departments, the only alternative to paying for a private violin or piano lesson would be to pay for a gifted child to attend as a boarder at one of the specialist schools. Seen in this context, the subsidy of first rate local private teachers is both a sensible and an economically sound investment.

71. **We believe that the recommendation that we made in relation to primary school children should apply equally to secondary school children, and that LEAs should draw up panels of local**

instrumental teachers, whom they consider suitable to teach in music centres and to give private lessons to children sponsored by the LEA. A scheme of this nature already exists in France. Those musicians who wish to be placed on the list of eligible teachers at the various conservatoires and state or municipal music schools take part in the annual Concours National Centralisé. The jury hears them teach both experienced and inexperienced pupils, and those who pass the audition are granted a certificate.

72. One of the most important developments of recent years has been the establishment of more local out-of-school music centres. The 1966 Report *Music Centres and the training of specially talented children*, published by the Standing Conference for Amateur Music, defined the two-fold purpose of Music Centres as providing a focal point for music teaching, especially for the peripatetic and part-time staff, and a resource centre for individual music tuition and organised group music-making during and outside school hours. The report defined the ideal centre as purpose built and separate from other school buildings, with a hall for rehearsing a full symphony orchestra and large choir and for chamber concerts, a library, sound-proofed practice rooms with good acoustics, instruments, tapes and records and some reproduction equipment. The report identified 34 such centres as existing in 1966 although these include adult education centres and those attached to technical colleges and colleges of further education.

73. This Enquiry circulated a questionnaire to members of the Music advisers' National Association to determine the extent of Music Centre provision in 1977. From the replies received it appears that almost all LEAs have Music Centres although their functions differ. Few are purpose built – the majority using ordinary school buildings outside normal school hours and at weekends. In some areas the Music Centre is primarily the administrative headquarters of the peripatetic and part-time music staff. In some areas it provides the only instrumental tuition available. In others it functions over and above the provision of full-time music teachers and peripatetics in the schools. In some LEAs the Centre makes provision for both gifted and talented pupils such as ILEA's Centre for Young Musicians which caters for 200 children. In other areas, particularly those with access to Junior Departments of Music Colleges, an award system is operated and the high-flyers go to these as Exhibitioners. In other areas the Music Centre functions as the

base for corporate music making where the youth orchestra, choir and brass bands rehearse. The majority of centres are staffed by the full and part-time peripatetics who teach in the schools and only a few take advantage of professional players as Visitor Teachers, although in at least one case a string quartet is retained both to give recitals and to teach in the Music Centres in the Authority.

74. Since 1966 the provision of Music Centres by Local Education Authorities has become part of the general pattern of music education, and is being expanded although hampered by the shortage of money available for building projects. Replies to our questionnaire were received from nearly 40 LEAs covering nearly 3 million pupils (about 30% of the school population). Between them they had established some 200 music centres which were attended by about 1% of all their pupils. About one third of the LEAs catered predominantly for older children, but in the remainder about as many children aged under 11 attended as children over 11. For children of both primary and secondary school age, Music Centres provide opportunities for talented players to meet together for ensemble work and pursue the general musical studies that the ordinary school, because of its obligations to all its pupils, is unable to provide. The centres can also ensure continuity in instrumental tuition and support for children moving from primary school to secondary school. Music centres usually organise courses in all instruments and provide orchestral experience. Some of them operate regular orchestral rehearsals, whereas others favour ensemble work in sections. The attendance at one of these music centres (providing the teaching is of a high standard) together with encouraging parents, a musically lively day school, and ample opportunity to practise will enable many children to acquire excellent musical training. **We strongly recommend authorities to expand, or where appropriate to create their own network of evening and weekend music centres.**

75. Nowadays, most LEAs run school or youth orchestras for their best players and there are youth orchestras drawn from the independent sector as well. This movement was commented on in *Making Musicians* and we should like to add our praise for the high standards these young players often achieve. However, the dangers of forgetting that a youth orchestra is basically an enjoyable educational activity can be insidious. Children can be exposed to the rigours of orchestral tours of professional proportions and to a demanding repertoire inappropriate to their

ability, all for the sake of the glory of the conductor or organiser. The real value of the youth orchestras for the young performer is in the detailed teaching by experienced coaches in the sectional rehearsals and in the full orchestra sessions taken by professional conductors and other musicians experienced in the training of orchestras, just as much as in the excellence of the performance itself.

76. Finally in this section, another form of out-of-school training for gifted children is the junior departments run by the five London music colleges and also the Royal Scottish Academy and the Royal Northern College. At the Birmingham School of Music there is a junior department run by the LEA. Most of these junior departments operate only on Saturdays. Students are either awarded Junior Exhibitions by LEAs or else pay their own fees. **Where appropriate LEAs should make arrangements for the support and development of these departments.**

Independent schools
77. We cannot conclude a survey of the musical education available to children attending ordinary schools without referring to the number of well-known independent schools with a strong musical tradition. While independent schools may produce only a limited number of professional musicians, they make an important contribution to the musical life of the country and we were impressed with what we were able to see of their activities. Historically many of them have played a major part in the musical culture of Great Britain and our impression is that their commitment to music is growing rather than diminishing. Moreover, because many of them are boarding schools they are well placed to provide the kind of environment which the gifted child needs – time and the opportunity to practise without interrupting the curriculum and sacrificing other interests, as well as the company of the similarly gifted.

78. As examples of the way music is organised in independent schools with a strong musical tradition, we would like to cite a boys' preparatory school and a girls' public school. At the preparatory school there are 373 boys. Of these, 192 boys learn an instrument. Some of them learn more than one; so the total number of instrumental pupils is 242. All boys have class music lessons at least once a week. Quite a large number take lessons in music theory during break times. The total staff of the school is 25, and of these 2 are music specialists. In addition, there are 11 visiting instrumental teachers who work part-time. There is a very

wide range of instrumental teaching, covering every orchestral instrument with the exception of the harp and contrabassoon. There is also an orchestra of about 40 boys, and a choir of between 50 and 60 who have performed in various places in the area from time to time. With regard to the Associated Board Examinations, during 1976 43 boys passed practical examinations; these included one grade 8 pass on the french horn and several grade 7 and 6 on various instruments. A further 35 boys passed the theory exams up to, and including, grade 5.

79. At the girls' public school, which is a day school, there are 530 pupils aged eleven to eighteen. It is a school with a strong academic tradition: virtually all girls continue to university or other higher education. One music scholarship is offered a year at entry; two in exceptional cases. In addition to the school's Great Hall, which makes a good concert hall and houses a good organ and a grand piano, there is a separate music wing. This comprises a small concert hall, a music library and listening facilities, a large sound-proofed teaching room, sixteen sound-proofed teaching rooms and a music staff common room. There are 4 full-time music staff and 24 part-time. Music is taught for G.C.E. 'O' and 'A' level (6 periods and 3 periods a week respectively) and university entrance. It is offered as a classroom subject throughout the school; after the third year it becomes voluntary. About 300 girls learn one or more instruments in school, and about 100 with outside teachers. The standard is high. A few girls each year prepare for the diploma exam (L.R.A.M. or A.R.C.M.) and several girls take Associated Board Grade VIII each term. There are two orchestras (a training orchestra and a more advanced one), a string ensemble, two or three chamber groups are coached each term, and there are two wind bands and three choirs. In addition to these groups which are trained by the staff, the pupils themselves organise a good deal of music-making including a choir for assembly, music for drama and other activities. The numbers learning instruments in the school are as follows:

Piano	195	Flute	45
Organ	6	Clarinet	31
Harpsichord	2	Oboe	18
Violin	41	Bassoon	2
Viola	8	Trumpet	4
'Cello	15	Horn	6
Bass	1	Percussion	9
Guitar	37		

'O' and 'A' levels in performance

80. For many young musicians in the secondary school, the G.C.E. 'O' and 'A' levels often present grave problems and a crisis of decision-making. At the age of 14 when instrumentalists should be consolidating their technique and combating the doubts and disturbances of adolescence, the prospect of numerous 'O' levels and the strain of trying to cope with them and keep up practice at the same time can be daunting to young players of talent. For the gifted young player with a fairly certain future in music, it is sensible to keep the 'O' levels to the minimum required for entry into higher education. It would be even more sensible to introduce an 'O' level in practical music-making; an examination that consists of performance, with a viva on the pieces played, the instrument that plays them and related topics. This Committee of Enquiry has had numerous representations from all quarters of the music profession, including the Incorporated Society of Musicians, pointing out the anomaly that whereas there can be double 'O' and 'A' levels in classics, mathematics and science, and 'O' levels can be given for practical combined with theoretical ability in subjects such as carpentry, this is not possible in music. When the universities demand a high level of performance for students intending to take an academic course in music, it is still impossible for that student to obtain recognition for the amount of work and study that has gone into the acquisition of that practical skill.

81. **We welcome the fact that certain universities have accepted Associated Board Grade VIII, Theory & Practical, as an addition to 'A' level for entrance to a music course. We recommend that double 'O' & 'A' levels in performance and theory (written skills, history, composition) should be respectable, legitimate options in their own right; and that candidates should be allowed to take either or both. The University of London Examinations Council is proposing a new music 'A' level scheme to start in 1980, comprising practical, theoretical, and combined practical/theory examinations. We warmly welcome this development.**

82. To ask that the music student should be able to gain a double 'A' level in a subject so variously demanding as music, is only to claim for him the same options that exist for his contemporaries in other fields. We do not believe that the danger of over-specialisation would be any greater than it is at present for candidates who take double 'A' levels in, say, classics, mathematics or science.

The 16-19 year age group

83. By the age of about 16, young instrumentalists should know the nature of their commitment to music. If they are talented this is generally the appropriate age for them to concentrate singlemindedly on preparing for a career in music. Later in this Report we argue the case for an extension of the basic music college course to four years and for an increase in the opportunities for exceptionally gifted performers to pursue advanced studies. Without in any way wishing to detract from the force of that argument, we feel that for the average potential orchestral performer it is often just as important that full time professional training should be provided at 16 to 19. The years between 16 and 19 can be a crucial watershed in the musical development of a young musician and yet too often in the past it has been a period characterised more by neglect of, than by attention to, his technical needs. At the age of 16 it may still not be too late to rectify bad physical habits in playing. At the age of 18, if these bad habits have been allowed to go unchecked for 2 years, by the time the student enters college they may have become so ingrained that at best a great deal of time is wasted trying to eradicate them, and at worst lasting and irreparable damage is done to the performer's technique.

84. It is, therefore, a matter of the highest priority that 'preliminary' courses of full-time musical training should be provided where necessary to fill the 16-19 vacuum. Several courses of this kind are already spreading up and down the country under the aegis of a specially selected secondary school 6th form, more frequently of a college of further education or a 6th form college, particularly in areas where the local authority has a pool of first rate instrumental teachers to draw from. Again we draw attention to the exceptionally small number of students involved. One centre for a conurbation like Greater Manchester and two or three for Greater London might well suffice. We recognise that the present structure of the English education system makes it difficult for authorities to support transfer of 16 year olds to music colleges on full grants, but that is all the more reason for the individual authority here and there to take the initiative in sponsoring the sort of pre-college courses in music that have been pioneered, for example, by Clarendon College, Nottingham, Winchester School of Art, Huddersfield Polytechnic and Kingsway-Princeton College in London. The small size of many 6th forms is a serious problem for local authorities and the Department of Education & Science. **It seems to us that in**

any reorganisation of the education of the 16-19 age group, opportunities should be seized for provision of a small number of specialist courses in music, preliminary to full-time professional training.

85. It is important that these two-year foundation or preliminary courses should be clear in their objectives. In some areas they may serve as a convenient pool for bringing together those students who wish to do 'A' level music, but who, either through teacher or candidate shortage, cannot undertake preparation for the examination in their own schools. But their main emphasis should be on the preparation of performers for entrance to a college of music or a university. The advantages for students in these preliminary courses are considerable, both in the great emphasis on ensemble work that is possible and also the level of commitment and achievement that can be expected when many are intending to become professional musicians. The increased scope that is possible when dealing with 40-50 students of this type compared with the small numbers found in the average sixth form is obvious, as are the advantages of teaching aural skills, harmony and general musicianship in groups. It is also possible to offer a much more extensive curriculum than is usually possible in a non-specialist school, together with better facilities and equipment. There are also important implications for the music colleges in catering for the new breed of student that will emerge from these courses. As one distinguished string teacher at the Royal Academy pointed out 'The eighteen year olds will arrive on the scene, having mastered the basic skills and being used to performing with others.'

Disparities in LEA provision

86. To conclude our consideration of the training that is provided for young musicians by LEAs, we would like to record our anxiety at the disparities that exist between the provision made by different local authorities. This was very apparent from the replies that we received to a questionnaire that we sent to LEA music advisers. And even in LEAs where there is above average provision, there can be marked differences between urban and rural parts of the authority's area, particularly as far as visits by peripatetic teachers are concerned. Although it is greatly to be welcomed when an authority makes generous provision for music (perhaps because of the personal commitment of a director of education, or a music adviser, or one or two councillors),

it is hard luck for a talented youngster if he happens to live in an area where inadequate provision is made. **We urge the local authority associations to encourage their members to make provision for musically gifted and talented youngsters along the lines advocated in this Report. We are convinced that the financial implications are slight and that the benefits (not least to music in schools in general) will be great. It is more a question of imaginative rationalisation of existing resources than any unrealistic increase in expenditure.**

The specialist music schools

87. For the parents of an outstandingly gifted child of school age – and, depending on the precise definition, there are only about 5000 such children in the whole country or one in 2000 out of a total school population of about 10 million – a big decision has to be taken, often at a very early age, whether they should try to get their child into a specialist music school. There are really two decisions to be made. First, is a specialist music school right in principle for their child, and then *which* school, because between them the five specialist music schools that exist present a variety of different options.

88. In the course of taking evidence we encountered opposition to such schools on the grounds that they are at variance with the general education policy of the country. The opponents of such schools believe that the special treatment of a small number of children is elitist, and that at a time when comprehensive education is being introduced throughout the state system such schools impoverish the general life of the school community by removing such gifted children from it. We would not wish to support the most highly developed systems of specialised musical education practised, for example, by a number of East European countries, whose aim has been to create a structure for the early identification of talented children who can be intensively trained at residential centres, however much some people may envy and admire some of the remarkable successes they have achieved.

89. But within the British school system as a whole, however good the general provision of music education, we have already seen how difficult it is to sustain a high degree of specialist music training at the necessary level to ensure the full development of the most talented children. Teachers do not always recognise the demands of such talent and its realisation requires the early development of mental resources

and physical proficiency of a sophisticated kind, imposing special requirements for tuition and practice. Teachers who have the ability to achieve this are rare, so the geographical isolation of pupils and the most economic use of resources often points to concentration in specialist schools. It has been our experience in visiting these schools that the possession of such talent is overwhelmingly important to the children themselves, and they need the stimulus and friendship of others similarly gifted, and regular and frequent access to teachers who can understand their gift and who can help them.

90. **The broad arguments in favour of a specialist music education (which we endorse) can be stated as follows:**

i) There is close association with similarly gifted children who can provide the stimulus of competition and example.

ii) Orchestra, chamber music and singing are all part of the curriculum and not left to the rush of the dinner hour or the exhaustion of after school. The opportunity thus exists for developing real musicianship, as opposed to technical proficiency, through daily aural training, choral singing, training in theory, and wide discussion and listening.

iii) There are facilities for instrumental practice during the day. This is vital for most musicians and especially string players and pianists.

iv) Opportunities for performance are far more frequent and varied than in non-specialist schools.

v) Master classes are taken by distinguished musicians visiting the school.

vi) Sufficient elasticity of the timetable exists to meet the essential needs of the individual pupil.

vii) Provision can be made for boarding accommodation, which means there can be more time for music and, above all, practice within the environment of the school.

91. But on the other hand parents may well ask themselves whether the academic education will be as good as in a normal school, and what happens if the child fails to make the grade musically, and whether there is a danger that the education will be too narrow in terms of the development of the child's personality. Conversely, how will the really talented child fare in an ordinary school? Will the distractions of all the activities available in, say, a large comprehensive school weaken the

child's commitment to music? Will the child be able to devote enough time to practise and at the same time keep up with the rest of the class when it comes to 'O' and 'A' levels? And will the teaching available either privately or at school or at the Saturday music centre be of a high enough standard for the really gifted child?

92. We come to the conclusion that there are no automatically right answers and that it is a great mistake to be dogmatic. What may be right for one child will be wrong for another. As with so many things in education, we are convinced that the decision has to be made in the light of what seems right for the particular child in question. We spoke to one parent who was convinced that her daughter would never have got to Cambridge as well as becoming a professional performer, if she had gone to a specialist school, and to another parent who felt his son would never have realised his full potential as a musician if he had *not* gone to a specialist school. The choice, therefore, must be a personal one, but the principle of the existence of such schools is one that we heartily endorse.

Financing the specialist schools
93. As far as the specialist music schools are concerned, the outstanding need is not to provide more of them – an unrealistic aim in the present economic climate and in view of the small number of potential pupils involved – but the achievement of financial security for those already in existence. These schools are inevitably expensive to maintain. They have high staff/pupil ratios, and they require capital investment in expensive instruments, practice facilities and residential accommodation.

94. Basically, up till now they have relied upon fees and endowments; this seems to us unsuitable as a long-term basis for the essential contribution they make to the musical education of gifted children. There are two issues. The first is that no talented child, wherever he is domiciled in Britain, should be prevented from attending a school to which he has been admitted, because his local authority refuses to pay the fees. The other is that the schools need capital and recurrent finance on a regular basis. One possibility is for the schools to become direct grant schools, as the Yehudi Menuhin School already is. The other possibility, which many of us favour, is for the other specialist schools to become maintained voluntary-aided schools, where the local authority, or a

group of neighbouring authorities, recoup the costs of children drawn from outside the area on a normal basis, as with schools for the handicapped. We estimate that the financial effects of either of these alternatives would be to increase public expenditure on these schools by about a third. We strongly urge each school to seek such arrangements as seem to it to be appropriate.

95. **We see no reason why all five should not either become direct grant schools or be maintained by local authorities with expenditure on 'out-county' pupils recovered as it is for special schools for other purposes.* Currently there is wide variation in the level of provision by LEAs for children wishing to attend specialist music schools, so that some children of exceptional ability are not admitted because the fees cannot be found. Considering the small number of children involved annually, we feel that, (as permitted by the Education Act, 1976), such assistance ought to be available for all those pupils who satisfy the entrance requirements of the schools wherever they live.** The number of gifted children and the intensive nature of the experience dictates that these schools will necessarily be small. However, they must be able to cater for the general education of the children if their future career options are to be safeguarded. It must be possible for a child to move back into a non-specialist school with ease if that move is to take place within the context of the child's own personal development and not be stigmatised as a failure to fulfil initial promise.

The five existing specialist schools

96. There are five existing specialist music schools as follows:

CHETHAM SCHOOL OF MUSIC, MANCHESTER

Although this ancient foundation had a strong musical tradition, it was only in 1969 that it became a specialist music school, whose only entry requirement is that all pupils should be gifted in music. There are just under 300 pupils, studying a full range of instruments, 250 are between 11 and 18, and the rest in the small Junior Department. The School is co-educational with roughly half boarders and half day-pupils, though the boarding provision is being increased. The annual intake is currently about 40, chosen, in 1976, as the result of 250 auditions out of

---

* Under Section 13 of the Education Act, 1944, any of these schools can opt for voluntary aided status with all the benefits that it would bring (see para 24).

about 500 original enquiries. There are close links with the Royal Northern College of Music, the Hallé and BBC Northern Orchestras and the Henry Watson Music Library. Over 50 Local Education Authorities in England, Scotland and Wales are currently providing grants for pupils to attend the school, so that a large proportion of its intake comes from far afield. More than 80% of the pupils are supported by their own Local Education Authority.

YEHUDI MENUHIN SCHOOL, STOKE D'ABERNON, COBHAM, SURREY

The School was started in 1963 by Mr Menuhin to train gifted children. It is a co-education boarding school that provides a general education from the age of 8 to 18 and a first-class musical training from teachers who are themselves distinguished artists. The school is a small international community with only 42 pupils. Violin, viola, 'cello and piano are the instruments which are taught. The school is the only specialist music school to receive a direct grant from the Department of Education and Science as a centre of education for the performing arts. In many respects it probably bears closest resemblance to the East European concept of the specialist music academy, both in the intensity of the musical training and in the concentration of children of outstanding talent.

PURCELL SCHOOL, HARROW, MIDDLESEX

Previously the Central Tutorial School for Young Musicians, this school was re-named the Purcell School in 1973 and moved into its present spacious premises in 1975. The school is a co-educational day school of 100 pupils aged 8-18 with plans to expand to 120-150. The philosophy of the Purcell School is very like that of a choir school. But there are certain fundamental differences – for instance, there is no connection with a particular cathedral or church. The Purcell School is co-educational, and takes pupils through their 'O' and 'A' levels. Pupils are accepted in one of two categories: those with exceptional musical ability or potential (the choristers, as it were) who must pass the School's music audition; and those who are selected by interview and who reach a satisfactory standard in the school's general assessments tests. The first category will therefore be specialist musicians, who will devote a considerable amount of time to music. The second category, all of whom will be required to have some expertise on a musical instrument, will be there because they wish to benefit from the thorough musical training which the school provides. The fact that it is within easy reach of central London offers the possibility of a close link with one of the London music colleges and, as the school expands, we would like to see it establish such a link.

WELLS CATHEDRAL SCHOOL, WELLS, SOMERSET

Wells Cathedral School is an ancient choir school founded in the twelfth century. Today it is a large independent school with a strong academic bias, consisting of 610 pupils (360 boys, 250 girls) aged 7 to 18, 300 of whom are boarders, many the children of servicemen and other public officials. About 70 boys and girls combine a rigorous instrumental or choral training with general education. 20 of these are on a specialist performers' course in violin, viola or 'cello; 40 are on a serious course of training which can provide tuition in any of the main orchestral instruments: 16 are Cathedral choristers. The specialist performers' course in strings is run under the general advice of Yfrah Neaman. It aims at the highest professional standards combined with a general academic education. The 'serious' course similarly enables a musical training to be integrated with academic studies and can lead naturally to graduate studies in higher education. String quartets and the chamber orchestra are vital for the 'specialist' course; the school symphony orchestra provides similarly for the 'serious' student. The 16 Cathedral choristers receive a disciplined musical training within the English choral tradition, again integrated with general education. There are a further 200 general musicians who do no more than learn an instrument with individual tuition and have no special aptitude or professional ambition. Though Wells draws boarding pupils from the whole country and from abroad, it is something of a specialist school for the Bristol and West of England area and many day pupils travel long distances.

ST MARY'S SCHOOL, EDINBURGH

In 1972 St Mary's changed from a conventional choir school to a specialist music school providing intensive training for about 40 musically talented children as well as continuing its former choir school education for about 20 choristers. The age range is from 7 to 17, there is a boarding element to cater for children from the more remote parts of Scotland and the long term intention is to restrict the overall numbers to about 60. The development of St Mary's in the future will necessarily depend on its relationship with any new specialist secondary unit that may be established following the report of the Working Group set up by the Scottish Education Department to consider the education of gifted young musicians and dancers, but the present position is that the grant that St Mary's receives under the Grant-Aided Secondary Schools

(Scotland) Regulations (1976) is being phased out over a 6 year period and is due to terminate in 1982.

The choir schools

97. In addition to the specialist schools there are also about 30 independent choir schools. The common interest of choir schools, whether they are attached to cathedrals, collegiate churches or chapels, or parish churches, is that they educate boys who sing daily services in choirs. This tradition of choral singing in Britain is without parallel in the world. One group of choir schools consists of independent preparatory schools which accept pupils at about the age of seven or eight and keep them until they are thirteen. In these schools they have the advantage of being educated in small classes. A few of these schools are for choristers only, but most take in other pupils. The other group of choir schools provides education as far as 'A' level and university entrance. These are larger secondary schools with junior departments, where a chorister may in many cases continue his singing for longer, until his voice breaks.

98. Most choir schools accept both boarders and day pupils but many insist upon choristers being full boarders. It should be noted that a few are for day pupils only. Some also take girls, who participate fully in the general and musical life of the schools. The fees in choir schools are similar to those charged in other independent schools, but scholarships are provided for choristers which reduce the total cost considerably. Choral scholarships are awarded after voice trials which are held once or twice a year. Many choristers also learn to play an instrument, and in some cases two instruments (keyboard plus another). Those who decide to become instrumentalists clearly benefit greatly from the disciplined training that they receive as choristers. **We welcome the fact that some LEAs contribute towards the fees of those who have been awarded choral scholarships and we recognise the value of the training provided.**

Chapter 3
The music colleges

The principal music colleges

99. Most of the principal music colleges were originally independent foundations of nineteenth century origin, formed for the specific purpose of training performers at a time when instrumental and vocal technique was rapidly advancing beyond the scope of the talented amateur and musical general practitioner. Although today eleven out of thirteen of them are wholly maintained or receive a subsidy of one kind or another from central or local government, in London particularly the colleges have tended to remain outside the mainstream of higher and further education. We shall spell out what we see as the different problems of financial independence and security; of autonomy; and of intellectual and musical freedom because it is here that the crucial problems are to be found.

100. Above all, there is the real difficulty that about half the students of the colleges have by design or accident found themselves entering as potential teachers. With the decline in the school population and a significant reduction of this avenue of employment in the coming decade, we have had to give the most careful consideration to the appropriate size of this sector of higher education. We were greatly handicapped by the statistical fog in which the arts are conducted and **we support strongly the plea of our colleagues on the Committee of Enquiry into Professional Training for Drama and the National Study of Dance Education that the Government Statistical Service should turn its skills to a thorough study of the artistic professions.**

101. The music colleges fall into three main groups. First, there are the 5 London colleges, then the 4 colleges in Glasgow, Cardiff, Manchester and Leeds, and then those schools of music that have been incorporated into polytechnics and whose achievements are such that they should be considered alongside the colleges. In this last category there are three institutions – Birmingham School of Music, which was of course originally an independent institution, Huddersfield School of

Music, and Colchester Institute of Higher Education. In a category of its own, there is Dartington College of Arts. Finally, in addition to these colleges of music there are also the colleges of education, some of which (such as Trent Park and Bretton Hall) have music departments with more than 100 students. These colleges are discussed in a subsequent chapter. The 13 music colleges and schools of music may be briefly described as follows:

THE ROYAL ACADEMY OF MUSIC, LONDON

The Royal Academy of Music, which is one of the oldest institutions for advanced musical training in Europe, was founded in 1822. The present main building in Marylebone Road was built in 1910. It contains a large hall, a concert room and an opera theatre. There are also class and rehearsal rooms, seminar rooms and studios for private tuition, and a major expansion of these facilities has been completed. The Academy premises extend to York Terrace East where the Library is situated. Student numbers fluctuate between 600 and 650.

THE ROYAL COLLEGE OF MUSIC, LONDON

The Royal College of Music was founded in 1883 and the present building in Prince Consort Road was erected in 1894 on a site granted by the Royal Commissioners of the Great Exhibition of 1851. The College now comprises two concert halls, two libraries, an opera theatre, an electronics studio, an instrument museum and a large number of teaching studios and practice rooms. A new extension was completed in 1964 and the dressing and rehearsal rooms associated with the opera theatre have recently been re-built and extended. The College has a total of about 650 students.

TRINITY COLLEGE OF MUSIC, LONDON

Trinity College of Music, founded in 1872, quickly established itself in all fields of musical education, and developed an international reputation by pioneering a world-wide system of graded examinations. The revenue from these examinations makes an important contribution to the finances of the College. The College holds the freehold of its site in Mandeville Place, London W1, and has, additionally, over 40 studios in its nearby Annex. The lack of a large hall, however, means that choral and orchestral activities must be held in outside venues. The College has about 350 full-time students and since the emphasis is on the training of instrumental teachers, the majority of students are on the three-year graduate diploma course with a limited number being trained as performers.

The deficiency grant

Since 1975, the above three colleges have negotiated a deficiency grant arrangement with the Department of Education & Science, whereby the DES agrees to meet any deficit between the colleges' income and budgeted expenditures previously agreed between the DES and the colleges. This arrangement provides greater security for the colleges than had hitherto existed, but the present economic situation has unfortunately meant that the hoped-for benefits from the new arrangement have not yet, as far as the colleges are concerned, really begun to flow.

THE GUILDHALL SCHOOL OF MUSIC AND DRAMA, LONDON

The Guildhall School of Music and Drama first opened in 1880 in a disused warehouse in Aldermanbury, but in 1887 the Corporation of the City of London, encouraged by the School's success, included it in a series of educational buildings which were opened on the Victoria Embankment. The City Corporation, which still maintains the School entirely out of its own funds, decided in 1965 to locate it in the Barbican Arts Centre. The School moved to the Barbican early in May 1977 where it will ultimately be adjacent to the Barbican Concert Hall, with the London Symphony Orchestra as resident orchestra, and the Royal Shakespeare Theatre. The School is different from the other London Music Colleges in that it has over 1000 part-time students of all ages. Its full-time music students number about 400.

THE LONDON COLLEGE OF MUSIC

The London College of Music was founded in 1887 when there was a growing demand for greater facilities for music education. Originally the intention was to provide part-time tuition for amateur musicians, and to institute local examinations, but over the years there came to be a growing emphasis on training full-time students for the profession and now no more part-timers are admitted. The College is situated in Great Marlborough Street and the building includes 30 studios and practice rooms, a concert hall and reference library. The College, which is the smallest of the London colleges, is the only one of the principal music colleges that is not at present in receipt of aid from public funds. It has about 240 students.

Residential accommodation for students at the London colleges

[Transporting musical instruments, particularly the larger ones, can be a difficult undertaking and lack of suitable living accommodation near the London colleges is a serious problem, though there have been certain developments since 1965. The Royal Academy has acquired a property in Camberwell, Ethel Kennedy Jacobs' House, which has room for 60 students. The Royal College has the Robert Mayer Hall of Residence which can accommodate 40 students and also has a number of places reserved for its students at Queen Alexandra House in Kensington Gore. Also in Camberwell – some distance from all four main colleges – there is Henry Wood House which is shared by the Academy, the College, Trinity and the Guildhall and can accommodate 75 students. However, the total number of residential places that the London colleges have available to them amounts to only about 200 for a total full-time student population of 2300. **In our view this should be trebled, for the reasons given in paragraphs 151-153. We recommend that there should be an immediate attempt to house 400 music students in Central London, where they could be within easy access of their colleges, possibly by making use of surplus accommodation arising from closing down former colleges of education or other vacant accommodation considered unsuitable for normal family use. The ultimate objective should be to create a situation comparable to that enjoyed by university students.**]

THE ROYAL SCOTTISH ACADEMY OF MUSIC AND DRAMA, GLASGOW

The Royal Scottish Academy had its origin (as the Glasgow Athenaeum) in 1847, became the Scottish National Academy of Music in 1929, and assumed its present title with Royal recognition in 1944. As the national conservatoire of music in Scotland, it is unique. The School of Music is housed on a commanding site in the centre of Glasgow. It comprises a small concert hall, the Athenaeum Theatre (for opera), a well-equipped library, television studio, student common-rooms and a refectory, as well as a considerable number of teaching and practice rooms of varying size. As a Central Institution of Higher Education, the Academy is financed directly by the Scottish Education Department and controlled by an independent Board of Governors on which both staff and students are represented. Plans are in being to increase the present capacity of 250 full-time students by the provision of a new building adjacent to a future municipal concert hall and civic theatre. About 35 residential places for women students are at present available in Gibson Hall of Residence.

THE WELSH COLLEGE OF MUSIC AND DRAMA, CARDIFF

The Welsh College of Music and Drama, which was formerly known as the Cardiff College of Music and Drama, recently moved into new buildings in the Castle grounds, Cathays Park, near to Cardiff's city centre and the university. The new premises include a studio theatre, teaching block, studios and practice rooms, and a large concert hall will soon be added to complete the complex. The College is maintained by the South Glamorgan Education Authority. It has 150 music students pursuing advanced courses.

THE ROYAL NORTHERN COLLEGE OF MUSIC, MANCHESTER

Perhaps most significant in that it is a new college designed as a model for the 1970's and 80's, there is the Royal Northern College which was formed in 1972 by an amalgamation of the Northern School of Music and the Royal Manchester College of Music. The new buildings comprise an opera theatre, concert hall, recital room, lecture theatre and extensive library. The college has purchased Hartley Hall, a former Methodist College, as a hall of residence which accommodates 200 students. The College is unique among the principal music colleges in that the basic course that it offers is a 4 year graduate course. The college is supported jointly by four local authorities – Manchester, Salford, Cheshire and Lancashire. It has about 400 students.

CITY OF LEEDS COLLEGE OF MUSIC

In 1965 Leeds Education Committee decided to develop its music centre to fulfil the function of a college of music. A full-time director was appointed and in 1966 the first full-time course was inaugurated. In evening ensembles, students have the advantage of working alongside a flourishing musical life which has developed from the adult evening classes, in which all traditional instruments are taught. The College has excellent facilities for study and practice, including an extensive library, aural laboratory and recording studio. There are approximately 150 full-time students.

BIRMINGHAM SCHOOL OF MUSIC

Birmingham School of Music was originally part of the Birmingham and Midland Institute, having been formally constituted in 1886, but is now a constituent part of the City of Birmingham Polytechnic. The new building, opened in 1973, is next to the Town Hall which is the performing home of the City of Birmingham Symphony Orchestra. The School has excellent teaching and practice rooms, as well as a listening and recording studio, a recital hall for over 250 people and a rapidly expanding library. Tuition is given to about 170 full-time students, plus about 160 students from other higher education establishments and about 100 part-time students.

HUDDERSFIELD SCHOOL OF MUSIC

The Huddersfield School of Music, which was founded in 1948 as a department of the College of Technology and is now part of the Polytechnic, was the first state supported institution to provide a full-time music education for students of 15 and over. To provide for expansion new premises were built in 1966. These contain a recital hall, lecture rooms, teaching and rehearsal studios, practice organs and a large recital organ, practice rooms and an extensive music and record library. It has about 280 full-time students.

COLCHESTER INSTITUTE OF HIGHER EDUCATION

Colchester Institute of Higher Education has been formed as the result of a merger between North East Essex Technical College and School of Art, and St Osyth's College of Education at Clacton. The School of Music is incorporated in the Faculty of Music and Art, and specialist accommodation includes a large auditorium, practice and teaching rooms and a music laboratory with audio-visual apparatus. There are about 180 full-time students. Residential accommodation is available at Clacton but not at Colchester.

DARTINGTON COLLEGE OF ARTS

The College is a part of the Dartington Hall Trust, and since 1976 has been assisted by Devon County Council. The Music Department has a purpose-built music school and is closely associated with the John Loosemore Centre for Organ and Early Music at Buckfastleigh. The Summer School of Music is administered as a Department of the College. The College is also the Arts Centre for the area. There are approximately 125 full-time music students with residential accommodation available for about 70.

102. The total number of students currently enrolled in full-time courses leading to a professional career in these 13 institutions is about 4000. For a detailed breakdown of the total of some 10,000 students taking music as a main subject, by type of establishment, see Appendix D.

Admission policies and the size of the London colleges

103. One question that is central to our Enquiry and to which we have given a great deal of thought is whether the music colleges, and particularly the London colleges, are training too many students bearing in mind the number of jobs available in music. That is not to say that an education in music is not an end in itself, which it most certainly is, but it is important to remember that the role of the music colleges is primarily vocational. There are great difficulties in arriving at a satisfactory estimate of the number of jobs available on account of the duplication that occurs between performing and teaching, and between having what is almost a full-time job in one field, but still working part-time in another. Moreover, when it is a question of matching training to posts, it may well not matter whether a post is part-time or full-time. A person spending half a day teaching an instrument and the other half bringing up a family still requires a full-time musical training, as does a person who spends part of his life as a cathedral or church singer and the rest as a gardener or shop keeper. However, we have arrived at a global estimate of 36,150 posts in Great Britain for which a musical training is required. (The details are set out in Appendix E.)

104. The same question of whether the music colleges were training too many students was one that exercised the Gilmour Jenkins Enquiry in 1965, particularly in relation to the London colleges. In paragraph 38 of their report, *Making Musicians*, our predecessors wrote:

'These colleges have traditionally held to the view that they should open their doors, as used to be done in the older universities, not only to the potential winners of first-class honours but also to the pass degree student, and indeed should offer their facilities to anyone reasonably gifted in music. This policy stems from the English habit of making no clear line of demarcation in music between the amateur and the professional. Under the pressure of modern conditions this will no longer serve, and the country needs a college or colleges specializing in the production of professional musicians of the highest standard. As a step towards this we should like to see the Royal Academy of Music and the Royal College of Music reducing their student intake so as to bring their numbers down within three years to approximately 400 in each. This would enable them to raise their standards for admission, to intensify the tuition and supervision given to a reduced number of students and to ease the pressure on accommodation for teaching and practice.'

105. In fact little reduction of the kind recommended by the 1965 Enquiry has taken place. In 1965 there were 673 full-time students at the Royal College of Music and there are 673 today. There has been a slight reduction at the Royal Academy of Music, from 753 in 1965 to a planned student body of about 650 when the current building programme is completed, but even this reduction is still far short of that envisaged in the paragraph from the 1965 Report quoted above. The Principals of the main London colleges concerned made it clear to us that they do not see the need for such reductions. They consider that there is little evidence of unemployment among musicians and, anyway, they see their role as not simply turning out musicians for the profession, but also as providing a higher education in music for those who want it.

106. Nevertheless the need for a reduction in the number of students being trained was urged on us most strongly by a number of those who submitted evidence. The principal arguments were that there are too many ill-prepared professional musicians for the available jobs; that the colleges were still catering too much for the amateur at the expense of the professional; and that the need to concentrate on the latter required that the available resources be used on fewer students. The colleges, it was argued, should concentrate on giving a more complete music training to a smaller number of really gifted musicians. It was put to us that they ought to select only those who have a real vocation for the

profession whether as performers or instrumental teachers. It would then be possible for college intakes to be more balanced in terms of the make-up of an orchestra, which at the moment is not always the case. The argument has strength.

107. There is, for example, currently a marked over-production of wind players. At the Royal Academy of Music it is necessary to take wood-wind and brass players through those parts of the repertoire that affect them in special sectional sessions because it is not possible to accommodate them all in the Academy's four orchestras. A former student at the Royal College, now a flautist with one of the London orchestras, claimed that out of the 40 or so flautists at the Royal College in his day only a handful could hope to get jobs in orchestras.

108. The London colleges really face two main problems. First, they are short of resources in certain crucial areas – they need more residential accommodation; under the deficiency grant system, their present recurrent income is not adequate to provide enough high quality teaching or pastoral care; their teacher training function is under threat. Secondly, a student on a performers' course not leading to a degree equivalent and without 2 'A' levels depends on a discretionary grant, which at the present time is an area of local government expenditure that is under great pressure, with some authorities even considering making no discretionary awards at all. Clearly the colleges would be in a much stronger position in their negotiations with the DES and local authority associations, if they are able to show that they are concentrating their training on a smaller number of really gifted musicians with professional careers in mind.

Courses offered by the colleges

109. At the present time, with some exceptions, most of the colleges offer two main courses – a 3 year performers' course with the possibility of an extension to 4 years in some cases, and a 3 year graduate diploma course. For example, the Royal Academy of Music and the Royal College of Music offer performers' courses leading to a completion of course certificate and the Licentiate of the Royal Academy of Music and Associate of the Royal College of Music diplomas respectively, and a graduate course leading to the Graduate of the Royal Schools of Music diploma. The GRSM diploma, which is common to both the Academy and the College, was rated as a university pass

degree but has recently been up-graded to become an honours graduate diploma. It is necessary for graduates to go on to take a one-year training course at a university institute of education or a college of education, if they are to obtain qualified teacher status and be recognised by the Burnham Committee as entitled to graduate rates of pay. The GRSM diploma does not itself cover classroom teaching techniques, though it does include instrumental teaching.

110. Most other colleges offer similar main courses. Roughly half of them offer a teacher's diploma or school music course (which must be followed by a further year of approved teacher training in order to obtain qualified teacher status), three of the London colleges (the Royal Academy, Royal College and Trinity) offer a London University B.Mus. course, a fourth (the Guildhall) offers a similar course in association with the City University, and three other colleges (Colchester, Huddersfield and Dartington) offer a BA course, validated by the CNAA. Four colleges offer foundation courses as a preliminary to full-time professional training and opportunities are available at most colleges for postgraduate or advanced study. The Royal Northern College offers a basic four year graduate course which is divided into two parts, two years of general study followed by two years of specialised training within the framework of one of six different schools of study. It also offers an associate course for performers, which is a diploma rather than a degree course.

111. The evidence that we have received leads us to believe that, as far as most of the colleges are concerned, the structure of their courses is unsatisfactory in three respects. They are not long enough for some students (particularly string players) to acquire the degree of mastery of their instrument and knowledge of the repertoire that the profession has the right to demand, they require almost immediate specialisation in the form of a commitment either to teaching or performance without the opportunity for a realistic appraisal of a student's career potential mid-way through the course, and, thirdly, there is the separation in the case of intending instrumental teachers between their course at music college, where they learn to play their instrument, and their year at a college or department of education where they obtain qualified teacher status.

112. On each of these three points we were presented with powerful

arguments that the present system needs changing. We were told that in most other countries it is considered that 5 years are needed at conservatoire level to turn out a performer of professional standard. It was put to us that the inevitable result of insisting on turning out 'trained' performers after only 3 years was to flood the profession with numbers of inadequately trained musicians who need a further period of study or else a period of orchestral training before they can be regarded as professionally competent. Certainly the orchestras complain that the training offered by many of the music colleges is incomplete. A side effect of this situation is that the orchestras, faced with a shortage of competent players coming out of the music colleges at the end of their courses, find themselves driven to signing up the more talented players even before they have completed their courses, and in some cases as early as the second year. This is a practice that the orchestras themselves regret and in a report which their Association produced in 1971 they urged that courses should be extended to 4 years and that their members should give priority to students who had obtained a completion of course certificate. The Principals of the London Music Colleges agreed that a 4 year course was an attractive proposition and that they would support it in the case of a substantial proportion of their students. They felt, however, that in certain respects the idea required careful consideration. Some provision would have to be made for students to leave at the end of their second or third year without stigma. After 3 years some students, in particular wind and brass players, were ready for orchestral playing and they felt that it was a pity to deny them this chance of experience and employment. Others might wish to continue their training abroad for a year or two without unduly protracting their total training period. Yet others might have reached the limit of their profitable instruction after 3 years.

113. As regards early specialisation, it was put to us that at some point in every musician's development a realistic appraisal of their career potential has to be attempted and it was argued that it was difficult to do this before a young musician had begun a higher education, except in the case of genuine 'high flyers' who tended to emerge at an early age. If a realistic attempt at appraisal of career potential is to be made then it is difficult to see how it can be done in a 3 year course with time still left for a change of direction.

114. Thirdly, on the question of the separation of the music college

course and the teacher training course on a consecutive basis of 3 years plus 1, the Principals were in agreement with the many witnesses who criticised the harmful effects of such an arrangement for those who intend to become instrumental teachers. It was put to us that the inevitable effect of this separation was that the year of teacher training was one in which students became out of touch with the profession and were unable to sustain their own personal standard of instrumental skill at the level they had reached at music college. In effect the separation meant that they learnt to play their instrument at music college and they learned classroom techniques in teacher training courses; seldom did they learn properly how to teach their instrument to others.

115. As we saw when we examined the training of young musicians while still at school, the greatest need as far as they are concerned is to raise the quality of instrumental teaching available to them. Talented children need good quality teaching from a very early age, particularly string players and pianists who should start no later than 7 or 8. Beginners need the best teachers, but under our present system of training the vast majority of children have very little chance of getting them. The initial stages of training are vital to the instrumentalist. If basic training is unsound, then faults become ingrained which are extremely hard to eradicate. It was put to us by a group of distinguished string teachers that a disproportionate amount of their time had to be devoted to getting rid of faults acquired at an earlier stage of training.

116. The young musician can only get the full benefit from his time at music college if he has a thorough foundation of musical knowledge and instrumental technique, but it appears that only a minority of students are thus equipped when they arrive at music college. In the past, the result has been that a sort of vicious circle is set up, with less able students tending to go into instrumental teaching at the local level, whether as peripatetics or attached to a school or music centre or teaching privately, and all too often reproducing their own shortcomings among their pupils. If there has been one theme that has occurred time and time again in the evidence that has been submitted to us, it is that performers should teach and teachers should perform. It is not simply that the experience of the current generation of performers needs to be made available to today's students or that the present generation of teachers need to maintain their own standards by the occasional pro-

fessional performance. The link between performing and teaching goes deeper than that. Rather is it that the process of self-examination that both must undertake when they take on the work of the other, acts as a spur to improve their mastery of their own principal professional skills. The teacher can often become a better teacher if he is able to perform, and the performer a better performer if the outlet and challenge of teaching is available to him.

117. What then are the implications of all these factors for the courses that our music colleges should offer? **First, we think it is necessary to draw a sharp distinction between training for a general class music teaching qualification and training to give instrumental lessons in schools and elsewhere to the minority of children who are attempting to learn an instrument.** Some colleges recognise this distinction explicitly; for example the Welsh College of Music has its Music in Education course and the London College of Music its School Music Course. Among the polytechnics, Huddersfield has two options on its Polytechnic Diploma course – option A for school music teachers and option B for instrumental teachers. Other colleges, however, do not make such a clear distinction. At the Royal Academy and the Royal College, for example, the origin of the GRSM course was as a course intended for both class teachers and for those instrumental teachers who wanted to be able to command a graduate's salary if they taught in maintained schools. But a tendency also developed for some of those who wanted to be performers to take the GRSM course in order to equip themselves to take other jobs in music if they needed to at any point in their performing career. This was especially the case with woodwind and brass players, where the demands of a performers' course were perhaps not as great as in the case of string players or pianists, and it was therefore possible for them to cope with a wider musical education during their 3 years at music college.

118. We believe that the time is now ripe to attempt some sort of rationalisation of the courses available to intending teachers. With the proliferation of courses for class music teachers that has taken place in other sectors of higher and further education in recent years, and in view of the falling school population, the role of the music colleges in training those who go on to become qualified class music teachers is already declining. It will decline even further, if – as we believe they should – the music colleges train fewer students and concentrate on

producing performers and instrumental teachers of a higher standard. We must reiterate here the distinction between a qualified teacher – one who is officially qualified to teach by virtue of completing an appropriate course – and a person who is fit to teach, say, the violin but who is not an officially qualified class teacher.

119. **We do not think that, as a general principle, training of qualified class music teachers should be made concurrent with the instrumental and general music training carried out within the music colleges. However, for those students who wish to raise the level of their performance to a high standard in order to teach their instrument as properly qualified teachers, and who may also be interested in the career opportunities thus open to them in school music, we think there should be one specially designated college that offers a four year instrumental teacher's course with a class teaching qualification built into the course, concurrently with instrumental training. We discuss this in more detail in our chapter on training teachers.**

120. In our view, the weaknesses in the structure of existing courses at some music colleges can only be remedied if greater flexibility is possible to take account of the differing needs of performers who want to be able to give instrumental lessons, of instrumental teachers who want occasionally to perform, and of class music teachers who may sometimes want to give instrumental assistance to their pupils. In this connection the proposals for a Diploma of Higher Education at the end of two years and a further two years' training to become a qualified teacher, which were recommended in the James Report on teacher training and education as an alternative to a standard honours degree, seem to us to be relevant to the training of musicians.

121. **We propose, therefore, that the music colleges should concentrate mainly on the training of intending performers and instrumental teachers rather than on those seeking a higher education in music or intending primarily to become teachers. All music colleges should offer four year first degree courses in order to raise the standard of achievement attained by students at the end of their course. For many students this will be a continuous four year course. The first two years should be a basic course normally leading to a Diploma of Higher Education. Students admitted to**

this course would normally qualify for a mandatory grant.* The second two years would lead to a degree or degree equivalent qualification that would usually embrace both performance and teaching skills sufficient to equip the student as a performer and to fit him or her to teach an instrument, but it would not carry qualified teacher status. Alternatively, it could be a pure performance course.†

122. It would also be possible for university students and for those who had taken a Dip HE at a musically-orientated Institute of Higher Education to switch into years 3 and 4 of the music college course if they wished to equip themselves similarly as a performer (or an instrumental teacher).‡ Conversely, it would be possible for those students at the music colleges who had completed the two year basic course and obtained their Dip HE, but who had decided that they wanted to be primarily qualified class music teachers rather than performers or instrumental teachers, to switch out of music college into a musically-orientated Institute of Higher Education in order to obtain a qualification as a class music teacher. Some might wish, too, at this stage to enter a university for the last one or two years of a music degree.

123. If this degree of flexibility could be achieved it would then be possible to satisfy the needs of:
i) the gifted performer who wished to concentrate solely on performance.
ii) the performer who wished to spend 4 years at music college and get a degree that would also equip him to teach his instrument well (to

* Admission to a Dip HE course does not necessarily carry with it a mandatory grant. Each student has to satisfy the conditions of the Awards Regulations relating to, for instance, previous attendance at a designated course and, more important, a Dip HE course is automatically recognised for mandatory grant only if it is in a maintained establishment (or one assisted by recurrent grants out of public funds).

† Special arrangements should be made to ensure that the gifted musician without any 'A' levels or equivalent qualification is not denied a grant for these last two years. In our understanding such a student after taking a Dip HE would be eligible for a mandatory grant for the degree course he or she was now entering upon.

‡ Full-time study for a degree undertaken after a Dip HE course carries an entitlement for a mandatory award for the residual period of the course (that is for a degree normally taking 3 years for the final year only, and for a degree taking 4 years for the final 2 years). Students undertaking part two after obtaining a degree elsewhere would not necessarily be eligible for a further mandatory award.

qualify as a teacher in schools a further year of teacher training would, of course, be needed).

iii) the instrumental teacher who wished to achieve a high level of performance.

iv) the university entrant who wished to take a further course for two years at music college to improve his performance, after either 2 or 3 years at university.

v) the intending class music teacher who wished to achieve a level of performance sufficient to enable him to give instrumental lessons as well.

vi) the occasional performer who wished to spend only 2 years at music college.

124. **We estimate that the net effect of the proposals in this section, involving as they do a reduced role for the music colleges in training those who go on to be class music teachers, would be to reduce the number of entrants to the music colleges by about a third, but to keep their numbers in total only slightly below those now there – say 3800 instead of 4200 – in view of the fact that more students would be remaining for a 4th year. But even though the music colleges would have a reduced role in training those who go on to become class music teachers, we think that it is important that they should safeguard and develop their role as centres of musical scholarship.**

Curricula for performers' courses

Instrumental training

125. By the time the student arrives at music college the technical foundations of instrumental skill should have been properly laid, so that it is possible for the colleges to concentrate on helping students to perfect their technique. But as we remarked in paragraphs 115 & 116, it appears that at the present time only a minority of students arrive at music college with an adequate mastery of technique. However, if our recommendations concerning the training of the potential professional while still at school and our recommendations on courses and admission policies at the colleges are adopted, we believe that standards at the point of entry into the music colleges can be raised significantly within a period of between 5 and 10 years.

126. In addition to helping students to perfect their technique, an important subsidiary role of the music colleges is to equip students with

the general musical skills that they need if they are to become broad-based musicians. There is no reason why the first two years at music college – that is the period of the Diploma in Higher Education in the course structure we are recommending – should not cover a fairly wide musical curriculum. Harmony, key-board harmony and figured bass, counterpoint, fugue, score-reading, ear training, analysis, musical history including a careful study of comparative styles, and ensemble playing can all now come into their own in group study. The Principals of the Colleges agreed with us that two hours tuition time per week was necessary in the principal instrument, and they felt that group teaching or the master class approach were valuable adjuncts to individual instruction, but should not replace it. We were particularly impressed by the system of double tutorials at the Royal Northern College whereby each student has one individual lesson and one group lesson per week, the equivalent of 2 hours per week individual instruction.

127. But if this level of individual instruction is to be achieved throughout the music colleges, then a lower student/teacher ratio will be needed than that at present existing in most music colleges. **Indeed we believe that the same arguments for a low student/teacher ratio apply in the case of the music colleges as in the case of the medical schools, and we therefore recommend that student/teacher ratios should be of the order of 5:1 (the ratio that applies in the medical schools) rather than the 8½:1 that is the norm in universities.** This would raise the cost per student but not, of course, to the level of medical students who require to use much complex and expensive equipment with technicians to service it, thereby greatly raising their costs above those of other students.

128. As regards a second study, conflicting opinions were expressed to us. The Principals expressed the view that basic keyboard skills for non-keyboard principal study players were of considerable practical advantage. They felt that principal study keyboard players should be offered the option to study continuo and accompaniment. Others took a different view and felt that it was difficult enough for players to acquire the skills they needed in one instrument, let alone two. Orchestral players themselves felt that second studies should either be taken more seriously or else abolished. **We feel that it is wrong to be too dogmatic on this matter. Clearly if a student is not benefiting from his second study, then he should drop it or switch to another instrument.**

Perhaps a second study is more necessary for the intending instrumental teacher than for a performer.

Orchestral training

129. One of the most frequent criticisms that we encountered in the evidence submitted to us concerned the orchestral training in most music colleges. It was pointed out that very few students become soloists, conductors or composers, and the majority become either orchestral players or instrumental teachers. But it is still the case that many pianists and string players are occupied almost entirely with training for solo playing, when it should be evident that they have no hope of a career as a soloist. The pianists would be better occupied learning transposition, continuo playing, accompaniment or coaching, and the string players learning how to play in an orchestra. Criticisms of this kind came not only from employers in relation to the recruits they obtained from the music colleges, but also from students and former students of the music colleges. To put them right would often require resources that the music colleges have just not had available to them, but whether or not these criticisms are justified, we must make it clear that they are made.

130. Throughout our Enquiry we have heard many references to a shortage of string players. Because of its importance we have given this question a great deal of consideration. What we have found is a complicated situation with several seemingly contradictory strands. On the whole, the orchestras are quite clear that there is a shortage of trained string players applying for the vacancies they offer. But when we looked at string playing in schools there appeared to be no shortage of good players there (for example, the Welsh County Youth Orchestras and the London Schools Symphony Orchestra), though looking ahead to the future it must be said that we also heard evidence from those who expressed concern for the future survival of string playing in many of our schools. Then there is the view of some of the Principals of the music colleges that the problem the orchestras face is that many of the best string players do not want to play in orchestras because to be just one of a large number of string players does not make playing in an orchestra so attractive as a career as it is for wind or brass players. Yet another view is that the string players (competent or otherwise) who apply for orchestral positions are insufficiently trained in what it is like to play in an orchestra, with the result that even potentially good players are judged inadequate by the orchestras.

131. But, if the standard of orchestral training in the colleges is to be improved then, in our opinion, two things have got to happen. First, orchestral playing has to be given a high priority within music college courses in terms of the amount of time allotted to it (this will have the benefit of raising its status which is also something that is badly needed), and secondly, the colleges must be able to make effective use of good coaches and conductors. Whether this is done by bringing in more outside conductors or specially appointing a conductor to the staff, will depend on the circumstances of different colleges. The Royal Scottish Academy, who at the moment have two members of their staff (one wind, one strings) responsible for conducting up to a week or so before a concert when they bring in an outside conductor, indicated that they would prefer to make a special appointment. In London that might not prove possible, in which case more money would have to be allocated to employing the services of first class conductors. One of the main reasons why college orchestras sometimes lack status in the eyes of students is that the quality of conducting does not make sufficient demands on them.

132. We feel that there should be more opportunities for students at the London colleges to come together and take part in joint ventures. The same thing should also be possible in other cities between music colleges and university music departments. It was put to us that, although students probably learn more about orchestral work from sitting alongside experienced professionals than from anything else, as a preparation for this they should be able to combine with their most talented contemporaries from other colleges in rehearsals and performances under skilled coaches and conductors of international reputation who are able to inspire students to achieve the highest standards. Master classes by distinguished artists from all parts of the world, when they visit London, could be an important part of such joint ventures organised for the most talented students. We think that the tendency of some professors to resist exposing their students to master classses by other musicians is a pity. If the students are sufficiently talented and have reached a suitably advanced stage in their training we feel that they can only benefit from the stimuli that such master classes could provide.

133. Finally with four year courses at the colleges, we believe that students should experience a wide range of music. When they leave music college, some young musicians will find themselves

working for a fair proportion of their time in the field of contemporary music rather than in a symphony orchestra.

Opera training

134. In the training of musicians there are problems which are particular only to singers. Many first class voices are discovered at a relatively late age and, unlike string players or pianists, this late start may often be an advantage because it can be positively harmful to start training a voice too rigorously before it has matured. Singers, even more than other musicians, thus frequently do not fit into the structure for qualifying for and obtaining grants. In particular they may not have the necessary 'A' levels and they may benefit from delaying full-time training until a time when their voices have matured.

135. Whether they start training at the age of about eighteen, along with music students generally, or whether they delay training until later, most singers are not ready to embark on full professional careers until they are in their middle or late twenties. They are consequently faced with the problems of maintaining themselves and obtaining grants for their training over an extended period and also of making the best use of their time over this period. What is clear is that Local Education Authorities need to be flexible in giving grants. They should be prepared to offer grants on a deferred basis and to consider sympathetically applications for awards to student singers, particularly mature students, lacking sufficient formal academic background. Moreover, when a young singer defers training and in the meantime takes a job to keep himself, then Local Education Authorities should be prepared to pay the fees for any relevant part-time training (such as languages – particularly German and Italian – acting, movement, make-up, costume and roles, as well as general musicianship) which he or she manages to undertake. For all young singers, but particularly for those who begin their studies early before their voices have matured, there is the problem of how to start a professional career. Evidence from the major opera companies stresses the need for them to have the opportunity to work with professional companies and we would like them to be able, after having finished their studies at the music colleges, to gain in-service training through periods of secondment to a company.

136. This would help to resolve the present unsatisfactory situation

confronting the student leaving college. He is currently faced with the choice of joining an opera chorus, which is useful work and professional experience, but which does not necessarily represent a good point of entry to the profession for someone with the potential for a solo career, or he can wait for the opportunity to take small solo parts which may never come. If this sort of apprenticeship were to become established the training role of the opera companies must be recognised. At present there is no intermediate contract between that of chorus and principal and it has been put to us that this should be established as a 2-3 year training position which would enable the young soloist to take progressively more major roles, to understudy and to learn the repertoire. This opportunity could be extended to 4-5 singers at any one time, but at present the extra money is not available within the companies to pay their salaries or those of the extra staff required to teach and supervise them. The advantages of a similar kind of arrangement, though on a more short-term basis, were fully set out in the Report to the Arts Council in 1976 of the Committee under the chairmanship of Sir Hugh Willatt on Advanced Opera Training in Great Britain. **The recommendations of the Committee included a scheme for the placing of ex-students or groups of students with opera companies: we endorse this proposal.**

137. Sir Hugh Willatt's Committee also recognised the need for some central co-ordination of the work of these ex-students for a period for guidance, and for training to supplement the experience and instruction which they would receive from the opera companies. For the young singer who may be faced with the temptation of undertaking roles as yet unsuited to the proper development of his voice, continued supervision and advice are most important and **we support the proposal for a centre for advanced studies for singers on the lines of the suggested National Opera Studio.**

Training composers

138. The true teacher of a young composer is essentially an understanding and perceptive guide. Of course he can, like any good teacher, endow his pupil with the tools of the trade: form, orchestration, the development of real aural command, to say nothing of specific practical techniques such as those involved in, say, writing for films or using electronic media. But in the final analysis, the true teacher of composition should be attuned to his charge, able to recognise and respond to

the inner creative forces in the younger composer, and able to draw out and encourage those elements that are ready for development. All this is fundamentally a private process. It is at most a communication on inner essentials between two sensitively attuned people. And as such it can develop and bear fruit wherever the necessary indispensable factors exist: privacy and patience, sympathy and stimulus, empathy and awareness. Such conditions can in theory exist anywhere. Certainly they can flourish in a university. They can be cultivated in a music college. They can succeed equally well away from any institution.

139. But there does then follow, and to a certain extent the two processes need to be concurrent, the point at which the new music must be brought to life in performance. No composer can really develop if his music is not played, if he is denied the opportunity to test his concepts against practical experience, to hear what he has written and to learn from that experience. This is the juncture at which collaboration with the performer becomes a practical, indeed a physical, necessity. This is often the biggest problem confronting the young composer. How is he going to have his music performed? It is now that the composer needs to find himself in a setting where he can call on able musicians to bring his music to life and it is important that he should be able to do so whilst his new work is fresh in his mind, while the problems which he has encountered in writing it are still actively with him.

140. So it is at this stage that the real advantage of young composers working in a music college or a university come to be felt to practical effect. Experience here often reveals an interesting further dilemma confronting a young composer with a choice to make. For whereas a really fraternal attitude by performers towards the young composer is often to be found at its most positive and constructive in a university, the performers are often not good enough or numerous enough to achieve all that they might wish on his behalf. By contrast, a music college is filled with able young players and singers, orchestras and even opera companies, but paradoxically the sense of collaboration is often less keen than in a university, and music college orchestras (and individuals) sometimes approach new music, including the new music of fellow students, with reluctance or even distaste – negative characteristics which are generally born of the performers' concern for their development as performers. Also, even in a university or a music college, the

preparation and performance of new music can be a costly business. It is inevitably somewhat so in both time and human endeavour, to say nothing of materials, to prepare multiple sets of parts and then to organise and hold multiple rehearsals, generally for a single performance of a work which then slips into obscurity having served the composer's essential requirement of constituting a temporary touchstone.

141. The admirable role played by the Arts Council in supporting commissions to composers should be matched by comparable support in helping the emerging composer to equip himself by practical experience to the point where he is ready to do justice to commissions. New music, which is written off as being inept, is often not that at all; it is merely the work of composers who have not had sufficient opportunities to test their mettle before entering the public arena. We do not ask young athletes to prepare for national events without first gaining local experience. **The young composer should be helped by the simple means of being performed as he develops. We recommend that the Arts Council of Great Britain should consider making more funds available for the preparation and playing of new music by promising young composers as soon as they emerge from full-time study.**

Training conductors

142. Much that has been written of the young composer may also be applied to the emerging conductor. Above all, like the composer, he is helpless without access to practical experience in performance, however sustained and thorough may have been the groundwork he has covered. The intelligent young conductor will seize every opening which may be available to him. He will pursue courses in conducting, whether over years in a music college or over weeks in a summer school. He will conduct any choir or orchestra which will let him, of whatever quality (and often he will learn most from working with the rawest material). He will get himself attached to an opera house as a repetiteur (if he can find one to take him on) and will recognise the value of conducting off-stage choruses or just coaching singers. He must be ready to gain experience in all directions, however improbable or unexpected.

143. The greatest difficulty is, as with the composer, that of acquiring practical experience. We believe that ways must be found to enable the conductor, like the composer, to gain initial and essential experience.

Although some expenditure in terms of providing talented young conductors with orchestras to conduct or ensembles to direct may in selective cases be desirable, there are also less expensive ways of achieving such aims. One is to make available more opportunity at postgraduate and post-postgraduate stages in the young conductor's career. The difficulty can often arise that he may have exhausted his grant entitlement in studying to be a good enough musician to embark on a career study as a conductor. The door to orthodox training as a conductor at a conservatoire may be closed to him on financial grounds. **The provision of a select number of bursaries or scholarships to overcome this particular difficulty is accordingly recommended. The annual bill might only be a few thousand pounds, but such provision could in practice play a crucial role in overcoming the danger that a gifted young conductor might be obliged to abandon pursuit of his art. We are not so rich in native young conductors that we should incur that risk.**

144. **A further proposal, designed particularly to be of mutual benefit to both conductors at the point when they have left a music college and gone to opera houses, is that a modest provision of funds should exist to enable opera houses to support one, or perhaps two, young conductors supernumerary to normal establishment.** It could be argued that this would constitute an extravagance, but in fact the actual cost would be slight and it could enable the opera houses to save money by not necessarily being obliged to buy in help in an emergency. Eventually, too, it could lead to more young conductors of appropriate calibre.

Training keyboard players

145. The reality of the situation is that the vast majority of students whose chosen instrument is the piano, the organ or the harpsichord will not be fortunate enough, probably by winning one of the major competitions, to embark on a major career as a soloist. Training at the colleges should reflect this reality. The course should give the student the opportunity to study the vocal and string repertoires. Training should be given in accompaniment, sight reading, transposition and playing from full scores, languages, style and some knowledge of choral training, dance movement and improvisation – all skills essential to the majority of keyboard players who become teachers and accompanists. Similarly training should be available for those wishing to pursue a

career as repetiteur, which within an opera company offers opportunities as a rehearsal pianist, coach and rehearsal conductor and is often the first step for those with ambitions to be an accompanist or conductor.

Staffing and remuneration

146. The status of teaching staff was a matter dealt with by the Gilmour Jenkins report in some detail. There is a marked difference in the pattern of staffing between the London colleges and those in Scotland, Wales and the English regions. In London the employment opportunities are such that few performers are prepared to take a full-time teaching job. The colleges in London are thus dependent for the major part of their teaching on part-time staff, who in many cases may only be prepared to teach for a very few hours a week. At the Royal Academy, for example, only a small minority of the staff do nearly all their work in the Academy, and the part-time teachers are divided between those who have an on-going agreement with the Academy and those who are employed on a casual basis. By contrast, at the Royal Scottish Academy full-time staff are in a majority and in fact account for over 80% of the total number of teaching hours. Historically, the main reason for this difference was the fact that in Glasgow there were fewer performing opportunities than in London and it was possible for performers to take a full-time teaching job and still undertake a little professional work as well. But even in Glasgow the situation has changed and we found that the Scottish National Orchestra had a number of players who would welcome more teaching opportunities.

147. Although the balance between full-time and part-time staff will be different in different parts of the country for reasons of this kind, we are convinced that it is important that there should be a balance. If a college fills too many of its teaching posts with full-time staff, there is a danger that its teaching will become out of touch with the mood of the performing profession and thereby of less value to its students. But if a college is going to rely on part-time staff for much of its teaching, then this can only work really effectively if it is possible to attract performers of the highest standard, and that means paying them a realistic fee. The Gilmour Jenkins report drew attention in 1965 to the consequences of failing to keep pace with fees paid for comparable work:

> 'The increases in rates of payment since 1939 have not been commensurate with those in other comparable occupations; the fees are now too low to compensate performers who devote time to

institutional teaching for the earnings they lose in other activities, nor have they adequate pension schemes. Two undesirable consequences flow from this. Those who have distinguished themselves in the profession and are still actively occupied as performers are not attracted by teaching. Those whose performing careers are behind them and who no longer can expect concert work to provide them with a substantial source of income, and those who have concentrated on teaching, are tempted to take more pupils, and therefore to teach for longer hours, than is good either for them or the pupils, and to blunt the edge of their zest by accepting pupils of only moderate talent.'

(*Making Musicians*, para. 36)

148. Although, as far as the three London colleges now receiving deficit financing from the DES are concerned, prospects for the future are brighter, the present situation is still no better, and in many respects worse, that that existing in 1965. In their evidence to us, the Royal Academy of Music Teaching Staff Association estimated than in 1975 the range of hourly fees paid to their members was from £2.90 to £4.75 per hour. Fees of that order mean that it is possible for a newly-qualified instrumental teacher working in maintained schools to earn substantially more per hour than his former professor, who might well be one of the finest teachers of his instrument in the country. But it is not just a question of rates of pay. Conditions of employment comparable with other teaching posts are also urgently needed. Teachers in the music colleges with a weekly teaching commitment, which in other educational establishments would entitle them to be permanently employed on a full-time basis, find that they have no comparable security and no pension rights. **We also felt that relationships between staff, principal and governing body in some of the music colleges still appeared to be rooted in the past and out of line with those prevailing in other academic institutions.**

149. Given the basis on which teachers are remunerated in many of the colleges, it is not surprising that the teaching provided comes in for a lot of criticism. The London colleges find it difficult to attract the best teachers and often do not get sufficient involvement from many of those they have. In the absence of satisfactory pension schemes the average age of their teachers is also high, with the result that a noticeable generation gap exists. This was clearly reflected in the answers

given by the musicians who completed our orchestral players question-naire. There was a consensus of opinion that there were too few first-class teachers in the colleges and that many of those in teaching were not suited to it but were motivated by the need to supplement their incomes.

150. In their evidence to us, the Principals of the London colleges said that they were greatly concerned at the low remuneration of professors in their colleges and at the fact that under the present arrangements they were unable to offer remuneration on a scale related to other higher education establishments and to offer comparable conditions of employment. They said that they would warmly welcome the payment of fees on a pro-rata basis linked to full-time salaries. **This we believe to be the correct approach and we support the proposal that the Incorporated Society of Musicians put forward in their evidence to the Houghton Committee in 1974. This involved calculating the hourly rate in accordance with comparable salaries elsewhere in higher and further education. Assuming a 10 week term and 20 contact hours per week, this would mean an hourly rate of 1/600 of the relevant annual salary* of a lecturer in a university, polytechnic or college of higher education, or between £8 and £10 per hour (in early 1977). This is two to three times the inade-quate rates now being paid and it is possible that this serious anomaly can best be remedied by an appropriate reference on the part of those concerned to Schedule 11 of the Employment Pro-tection Act 1975.**

The music college as a community

151. *Making Musicians* pointed to several factors that tended to make it difficult for students in London to engage in communal activity within the musical environment of their colleges. Perhaps the most serious of these factors is the lack of residential accommodation in London within a reasonable distance of the colleges, to which we have already referred. Since the Rent Act 1974, the supply of furnished flats has been much reduced. Even so, most students do manage to find accommodation with somewhere where they can practise, but the trouble is that in many cases it is too far away from their colleges and involves them in too much travelling. One regrettable aspect of students living too far

---

* Average salary of £5,570 or £9.30 per hour at end 1976. (UGC)

away from college is that it means that they tend to try and concentrate their timetables into 2 or 3 days a week and only travel to the college on those days. This inevitably weakens the identity of a college as a community.

152. The situation in London is in marked contrast to Manchester, where the Royal Northern College has obtained residential accommodation for nearly half of its students, and to Cardiff where there is also adequate student housing available. Where this kind of accommodation is available it means that a lot of impromptu chamber music is able to take place in the evenings and at weekends as well as a host of recreational activities of one kind or another, in which a large number of students can take part. Other advantages that the colleges away from London have are that it is easier to keep open for longer hours since commuting is not the problem for students and staff that it is in London and there is also a greater involvement of staff in the life of the college because of the higher proportion of full-time staff in the colleges outside London.

153. When the life of a music student in London is compared with that of an undergraduate at a university, the contrast is a stark one. At a university a wide range of activities are available. The undergraduate reading music may at the same time take part in drama society productions, write for or edit a magazine, or be an active member of a political club, as well as playing in the college orchestra or singing in the university choir. The student in a music college in London on the other hand is presented with a demanding specialist course, and virtually no other extra-curricular activity. He may be living in digs, as much as an hour's journey away from the college with little chance for practice. The result is that he may come into college for only a couple of days a week and, apart from playing in an orchestra or singing in the choir, will have little corporate life comparable to the clubs and societies that exist in such number at a university.

154. Another disadvantage of the present situation in which students at the London colleges find themselves is the lack of sufficient general tutorial advice of the kind that would normally be available in a university. It is true that some colleges (the Royal Academy, for example), allocate all students to a tutor as well as to a professor, but with the low level of full-time commitment that exists in the London colleges

such an arrangement can in no way be comparable to the amount of general tutorial guidance that other students get at a university.

155. **Career advice is another aspect of the tutorial relationship that is important in view of the highly competitive world in which the professional musician has to make a living.** Ideally this career advice should grow out of the general tutorial guidance that is given to a student throughout the whole period of his time at music college rather than simply be a sort of service that is provided to him just before he leaves. It was put to us by the ISM that over and above career guidance students should receive a training in career management and business studies while they are still at music college so that they will be better able to cope with the business side of managing their own careers when they are trying to establish themselves in the profession. We accept that the London colleges are faced with special difficulties in trying to provide this kind of service to their students, and in trying to make their colleges the focal point of a community of musicians with a sense of identity and purpose, but we feel that a higher priority should be given to trying to overcome these difficulties.

The future of the London colleges

156. In any discussion of the way the London colleges are financed it is necessary to separate the Guildhall School of Music and the London College of Music from the three colleges at present in receipt of direct subsidy from the DES – the Royal Academy, the Royal College and Trinity. The Guildhall receives a revenue subsidy from the Corporation of the City of London; it is now housed in a new complex in the Barbican; it is combined with a drama school; and, as well as running full-time courses, it also caters for a large number of part-time students. However, now that the School at last has a building with adequate facilities for the proper training of music and drama students, it is faced with the much higher costs of running the building. If fees are not to be raised to astronomical levels, a further subsidy is needed in addition to the £400,000 provided by the City. **The School has discussed the need for public funds in addition to those provided by the Corporation of the City of London and it could well be that it should link itself with the City of London Polytechnic or the City University in order to provide itself with a suitable basis for public subsidy.** The London College of Music, dependent almost entirely on its fee

income, also obviously faces problems with the present difficulties in getting discretionary grants, but its future is not directly a matter for public bodies to determine.

157. It is easy to list the problems affecting the London colleges but difficult to answer them. We have argued that the London colleges need extra recurrent income and some extra capital expenditure – above all for residence with some 400 extra residential places being needed. We have argued that the extension of their normal courses to 4 years is desirable; we would like them to admit fewer students for more intensive courses, closely related to employment opportunities; and, in this respect the severe reduction in their teacher training role is an inescapable element that has to be considered. **Taking it all in all, we think that it is desirable for music education and training in London to enter the public sector, as described below. We accept that this will require additional public expenditure, but this will be off-set to some extent by the reduction in student intake numbers and by savings in the teacher training sector. In our view it is unsatisfactory in principle that the form of state subsidy provided to the most eminent music colleges in the country, should be one of a guarantee against loss rather than a positive programme for the development of musical training and education. Instrumental music has been unduly kept out of the mainstream of higher education to its disadvantage. Now that the taxpayer is making a direct subsidy to these colleges as well as giving the indirect subsidy that is obtained from student grants and fees, then it is surely right that instrumental music training in London should take its full place in higher education, as in Scotland, Wales and in the rest of England.**

158. We do not specify the precise form that the relationship should take, but we are confident that in the changed conditions which we are postulating, where the colleges admit fewer students and concentrate to a greater extent on those who wish to train as performers or as instrumental teachers, it is entirely right that there should be a greater emphasis on the proper funding of the London colleges and that they should assume a more clearly defined place in the spectrum of higher education and training. **The Royal Academy of Music and the Royal College of Music should either become monotechnics maintained by local authorities or they should become colleges of**

London University. In view of its experience in training instrumental teachers, Trinity should be the one music college that
offers a four year course with a teaching qualification built in as
part of the course. (see para 175)

159. We strongly urge the two Royal Colleges and Trinity actively
to explore these possibilities. The benefits which would flow are
clear. First, the recurrent grant would be on a more consistent
basis and, probably in the long run, bigger; next, the students
would stand a better chance of getting more residential accommodation and they would have fuller access to the capital's student recreation facilities; thirdly, gradually, the colleges would
benefit from the standards of staffing and pay that are provided
elsewhere in the higher education system.

Chapter 4
The universities

University and music college

160. With the growing emphasis on performance in many university music departments in recent years, universities have now become an important training ground for musicians of all kinds. Whereas in 1965/66, at the time of the Gilmour Jenkins Enquiry, the number of students in university music departments totalled 730, by 1975/76 they had more than doubled to over 1700. Moreover, whilst the total number of university students has changed little in recent years, music departments have continued to expand; in 1975/76 for example they contained some 30 per cent more students than three years earlier. We give in Appendix F broad figures of first destinations of music graduates from universities in Great Britain and of students leaving a London music college. From these tables it is clear that, compared with the music colleges, the number of performers entering the profession from universities is small. Those that do become practitioners however make a distinctive contribution to professional music. The point was made to us by the Association of British Orchestras when they gave evidence, that university graduates tend to have a greater understanding of the problems facing orchestras and to contribute more to the life of an orchestra that those who lack the broader educational base that a university education can provide.

161. During the course of our deliberations, and especially when we were hearing evidence in various regional centres throughout the country, we gave careful consideration to the relative merits on the training offered by the music colleges on the one hand and universities on the other, in relation to different types of musicians and different performing skills. We came to the conclusion that the kind of performer who wants to live and eventually work in an environment given over entirely to the playing of music will be more likely to go to a music college. A university might be chosen by performers with a wider motivation, emphasising versatility, and by those who are more academically minded. It is impossible to generalise, since the instrument

concerned affects the issue so closely. The continuous training from childhood associated with stringed instruments or piano is more than likely to suggest music college for a virtuoso. One eminent string teacher told us that she would no longer take university students as pupils because they were not able to put in enough practice time. But the distinction cannot be made in terms of instruments; rather the suitability of the student for academic study, and the timetable this implies.

162. Students who opt for music at a university do so for a number of reasons. Most of them are good at music and wish to pursue it further, as they would with any other subject. This can lead to a career either as a performer or in teaching, publishing, administration, musical journalism, or the recording industry. Unless it is obvious that these students are specially gifted as performers, they may not know which career option they are going to follow, or even whether they are likely to work outside music altogether. Often these different activities will be mixed, and here the flexibility of university training is an asset. For these students, and those whose main interest is musicology, their choice of university is more obvious than for intending performers and composers.

163. At present it seems to be fashionable for composers to want to go to university rather than music college, but this was not always so, nor need it necessarily be so. Certainly, there may be more opportunity for a composer to specialise in composition for some years at music college and to have his work performed (which is vital to any composer), but on the other hand he may find that the wider world of the university provides more of the stimuli that he needs to express himself in music. We have to remember that composing is not a career like performing where a player is trained for life and may do nothing else. Composers, like singers and conductors, need long development. One solution is for composers to follow a university degree with a period at a music college, here or abroad. The talented – and the lucky – will obtain fellowships or grants, which are as necessary for the composer as for the advanced performer, but these are few and highly competitive.

164. The performer who opts for university, in addition to being academically minded, will probably be one who has reached a sufficiently high standard technically at the age of 18 to be able to decide to com-

plete his training in music in a wider environment than that of a music college, where he can learn about the structural and historical aspects of music and where there is some research going on. All this he can do within the wider context of the world of the university. The philosophies of different university music departments naturally vary. But most of them regard musical performance as an integral part of the study of music at all levels. One university estimated that almost all the students entering their undergraduate course in the last 6 years had grade 8 on one instrument, and about half on two instruments. Generally students will not be accepted without a good standard of performance on at least one instrument. Arrangements may be made for students to continue study with specialist teachers, and they usually have a chance to give a recital for their final examination. This integrated pattern of musical training has been particularly associated with the newer universities. There is often sufficient flexibility in teaching arrangements for an outstanding student to be sent to an appropriately advanced teacher, but this student will still have to fulfil the academic requirements of the course as a whole. Universities also aim to develop the performing skills of those who will not become fully professional performers, in the belief than an essential component in the study of music is its performance. This remains true in the field of musicology, since it would plainly be pointless to research into unknown music if there were to be no prospect of its being heard.

165. What is lacking at a university, is a large body of students all training from the start to be professional performers and therefore sharing a well-defined aim; though the best university communities do provide, in common with the music colleges, plenty of opportunities for performance. In universities the scope may depend more on private enterprise and less on professional direction. Students there are able to find out about rehearsing, managing and presenting operas, musicals, plays, multi-media events. The opportunity for the student's own initiative in such matters is virtually endless, all in the context of three or four years on a grant. Performers of distinction have emerged from this kind of stimulating background – often to continue study at a music college – not to mention the contribution of universities to the ranks of administrators, BBC producers, critics and impresarios. Such people may have developed their own musical tastes in a university environment and have gone on into jobs where they have the chance of moulding the tastes of a much wider sector of the community.

The size of the university sector and the courses available

166. There are 32 university music departments in Great Britain with a total of about 1700 students (see Appendix G for details). At most universities students can choose between a single honours music degree where their course is almost entirely music, or a combined honours course where music is one of two, three or even four subjects studied. These courses sometimes provide opportunities for relating their subjects, but even in the inter-disciplinary situation music is integrated with performance. At a number of universities the career expectations of music graduates are increasingly taken into account. Tonmeister courses and joint degrees with music and electronics, physics or computer studies, relate to the technical side. The fields of administration, publishing and management are also reflected in some music degrees.

167. A study of university prospectuses shows that the old academic study of music has virtually disappeared. The boundaries have been broken down on several sides: modern music is increasingly popular, thus encouraging composers; early music is enjoying a boom, reflected in concerts and records in the outside world; music outside the European tradition is increasingly studied, and there is some representation of popular music and jazz. A special kind of performance is involved in the field of live electronic music: several universities now have electronic studios at the disposal of the music department, again attracting composers, and some of the music colleges have programmes in this field too. Another major justification of university departments of music remains their role as a forum for specialised work leading to research, performance, and publication. In this respect recent cuts in grants and increases in fees resulting in the constriction of post-graduate provision are likely to diminish the specialised work done by faculty and research students. This is relevant to this Report since higher degrees in some institutions involve an element of performance, in some cases arising from original research.

168. There has sometimes been criticism of the continued growth of music departments in universities since the 1965 report. Some universities with Directors of Music have added teaching staff and accepted music students. Declining school rolls now mean that fewer music graduates will go into teaching, but some of the other avenues of employment already mentioned will gain in importance. We accept the

educational value of music as a subject on a par with, and probably superior to, many other subjects traditionally regarded as a means of acquiring a trained intellect. This view is unfortunately not yet general in universities or in educational thinking in this country today. **In view of the contribution of music towards building an educated person, and its demonstrable popularity and relevance, and in view of the severe contraction of music courses in initial teacher training, it seems likely that applications to read music either as single or joint honours at universities will continue to increase. We strongly urge university music departments to follow the advice of the University Grants Committee, in its 1975-6 Report, and to seek to establish links with each other, and with institutions outside the university sector, such as polytechnics and institutes of higher education, in order to make the best use of their resources.**

169. Now that 32 universities have departments of music, and most have Directors of Music with the function of organising musical activity on the campus, they are in a position to make a contribution to the musical life of the regions in which they are situated. As a focus for musical life, university music departments are of great value, although the emphasis each one places on this aspect will vary. Those universities sited in larger cities present an active concert life on both amateur and professional level. And those remote from big towns have fulfilled a special function in providing music where little existed before. Collaboration with local musical societies is also particularly important for concert promotion. All these functions are of value to the musical profession both in training and in providing jobs for those trained. **Some of the universities work closely with the Regional Arts Associations. These bodies with increasingly devolved power should be encouraged to work more closely with universities as natural centres of public performance within their regions. The universities too should be encouraged to work with such bodies and to ensure that their programmes bring the work of the living composer to a wider audience within the areas where they are located.**

Links between universities and music colleges
170. Links between universities and music colleges can take two forms. First there are the physical links that may exist in those cities where there is both a university and a music college. Then, there is the mobility that there ought to be between the two types of institution which

makes it possible for a limited number of students to go on to music college after two or three years at university or vice versa. In some cases this informal traffic is being recognised by formal course arrangements. It is already the case that a few of the most academically gifted musicians at those universities emphasising performance often go on to a music college to prepare themselves for entry into the profession. However, it can be difficult for students who want to do this to get grants. We believe that it is regrettable that this should be so, particularly since the number of students seeking to go on to a music college is very small. **We think that, provided our proposal for a two-part, four year, course at the music colleges is accepted, for the performers that come out of a university music department the normal form of post-graduate study should be at music college rather than a further year within their university. We recommend that this should be encouraged by those making post-graduate awards, who have, not necessarily undesirably, been reducing their emphasis upon awards for postgraduate research. Similarly, we also suggest that for a number of students who have completed two years at a music college, and taken a Diploma of Higher Education, it will be appropriate to go on to university to take the last two years of another degree. This is easiest in those universities which have a Part I and a Part II degree structure. It is a development we wish to encourage.**

171. As regards the links between university music departments and music colleges in the same city, we were surprised to find that they are not as close as they might be. In Manchester there is a joint course arrangement with a 4 year commitment between the Royal Northern College and Manchester University, and in London students may be accepted for a 3 year course at the Royal College, the Royal Academy and Trinity leading to a London University B.Mus. degree. Students taking these courses have the status of internal students of London University and some of their work is done at colleges of the University. The Guildhall School of Music has a similar arrangement with the City University. But even in London and Manchester these links could be closer and there are other cities where links are very slight indeed. We think this is a great pity, because for the most part the cities where university music departments and colleges exist together are those with a vigorous musical life and often the homes of orchestras and sometimes opera companies as well. **In such cities there is great scope for**

a healthy and stimulating interchange between colleges and universities involving musicologists, analysts, performers and composers. It should be possible to develop highly flexible courses which give individual students the best sort of balance in their musical education. With the financial resources of our universities and colleges coming under great pressure, we believe it is essential to make the most efficient use possible of the facilities available.

Chapter 5
Polytechnics, institutes of higher education and the training of teachers

The present position and future requirements

172. This Report was being written as many of the colleges of education were being closed down or merged. The training of teachers, which originated with so much else mainly in the 19th century, was altered in the early 1960's by the extension of the 2-year course to 3 years, and by the introduction of the Bachelor of Education degree. The great growth in the number of students took place from the late 1950's, and it was suddenly accelerated, until a system was created which was 7 times larger than that which had persisted for many years, with a total of about 160 colleges of varying size. But now, the biggest single influence, not only in education generally but also in music education, is the fall in the number of school children of compulsory school age by nearly 2 million by the end of the 1980's. As most professional musicians earn some or all of their incomes by teaching, the contraction of the school system profoundly affects the career structure in music, and the role of all institutions that train musicians.

173. The contraction to a system of initial teacher training less than half as large as it was in the late 1960's, is not a reversion to the simplicities of the 1950's but a widespread general upheaval. Some colleges have been closed or shortly will be. The greater part of the remainder have been merged with polytechnics, or turned into institutes of higher education, or (in a few cases) merged with universities (Exeter, for example). The new system is not the old system writ small. It is very different. Over the next decade there will only be about 17,000 new teachers a year, compared with 30,000 to 40,000 a year during the period 1965-75; a quarter of them will be graduates in the general sense, and the remainder holding the Bachelor of Education (or equivalent) degree. Of these only between 700 and 800 will be music specialists. In the next ten years, the number of newly trained teachers will rarely reach 1 in 30 of the total number of teachers. Important though their training is, they will be a drop in the ocean compared with existing teachers. A large primary school of 10 teachers will get a newly-trained

teacher possibly once in three years. **Any change in the quality of the teaching of music must thus largely depend upon the up-grading of existing teachers.** We accept that in 1976, music was a 'shortage' subject, with about 300 posts for specialists filled by non-specialists. In our judgment, this shortage will diminish as the tide of pupil numbers recedes.

Providing the training that is needed

174. Our predecessors, the Gilmour Jenkins Enquiry, drew attention to the fact that in 1965 about half the students in the principal music colleges were intending class teachers. We have explained that at the age of 18 it is probable that a number of promising instrumentalists choose to train as teachers because it seems a safer course and because it guarantees a mandatory grant. We have made proposals that courses at music colleges should carry mandatory grants and should divide at the end of the second year – almost imperceptibly for most students, comparable perhaps to the division between Part I and Part II of the honours degree, but definitely for those students who then want to become qualified class teachers, or who want not to be principally performers. We accept the argument of our predecessors that all intending teachers should not be hived off at first, because at 18 it is difficult for people to be sure how good they are potentially and how committed they are as performers, and secondly because some qualified class music teachers ought also to be excellent instrumentalists. **But, as we have said in Chapter 3, we do not think the main job of the music colleges should be training those who intend to become qualified class teachers; rather we would wish the promising instrumentalists who are going to be qualified class teachers, either to enter teacher training courses elsewhere, with special arrangements for instrumental teaching, or for those who leave the music colleges with a Diploma of Higher Education after two years to enter the other colleges at that point.** The present widespread upheaval in the organisation of teacher training, triggered off by the projected decline in the school population, opens up the practical possibility of implementing this proposal.

175. In our view, there is an urgent need to upgrade the training and status of instrumental teachers. To some extent, of course, they overlap with qualified class music teachers, but in principle their roles are different. We have already suggested that most per-

formers should also learn to teach their instrument. For those good instrumentalists who wish to become qualified class teachers, then we recommend that Trinity College of Music be specially designated as providing a teaching course leading to qualified teacher status as a class music teacher and also as an instrumental teacher, with musical and pedagogical training running concurrently. One college of higher education should also be similarly designated for this purpose and its staff and facilities suitably developed. In view of official policies, Trinity College would have to be closely linked to an existing teacher training institution, and its student numbers included within the totals already determined for initial teacher training. This will require positive steps.

176. The position of teacher training in the future may be briefly described as divided between initial training and in-service training, with the latter (for the first time) by far the more important and difficult task. We shall discuss this later. Of the 17,000 newly qualified teachers in England and Wales each year, nearly 800 or so will be trained musicians.* If our proposals are accepted, about a third of this 800 (250 or so) will be music graduates from the universities, and about half will come from Bachelor of Education courses having taken music as a main subject; additionally, about 100 will come from Trinity College, but only a small number (50 or so) from the other music colleges (see Appendix H). Initial training for music (that is non-Bachelor of Education graduates) will take the form of a post-graduate teacher training period.

177. This is particularly relevant to the graduates of the music colleges, since much of the criticism of teacher training has focussed on the discontinuity where circumstances often make it difficult for instrumentalists to continue to study their instruments. After three or four years mainly learning an instrument, they have a year in a university education department, or on a polytechnic or college Post-Graduate Certificate of Education course, consisting of courses in education, philosophy, sociology and other topics, with teaching practice, oriented towards the classroom. The same is true of music graduates from the university, though in their case the executant side may be less significant than for the ex-music college student.

* This is the official figure for 1981. It may well be too high for the remainder of the 1980's.

178. **As far as the Bachelor of Education students are concerned we think it essential that future class music teachers should be drawn from colleges which have a strong commitment to music.** In the case of music, students entering a college will already have achieved a high musical standard and during their subsequent training they should certainly be enabled to continue at least to maintain their standard as musicians while broadening out their music contribution in a good environment. It is essential that any institution training music teachers should also have music as an important element in its own higher education programme. It should also see music as making a major creative contribution to the life and work of the community, as well as relating to other arts within the college and in the neighbourhood. Facilities and resources should be of a high standard, and the college should offer a genuine example of the musical atmosphere which it is hoped the students would go on to create once they became teachers.

179. Their training must require, as a minimum, instrumental, choir and orchestral practice; music theory and history; and a wide musical culture as practitioners and listeners. They will help to create the musical atmosphere of the schools; they will provide the means by which the talented will be identified and helped; it will be they who liaise with the peripatetic teachers, the music centres, Saturday music schools, county youth orchestras, and who will be responsible for drawing the attention of the authorities to the special needs of talented and gifted children. It follows, therefore, that while most if not all colleges where teachers of any kind – especially primary school teachers – are trained should be able to provide music 'minor' options, since many non-music specialists will rightly want to 'do' music (as they do history and mathematics), a small number of colleges must specialise in the complex and difficult task of training music teachers.

180. No extra expenditure will be involved. A large number of colleges are being closed or merged. There exist, in relative abundance, in buildings up and down the country, special studios, theatres and concert halls, musical equipment and instruments and qualified staffs. It is essential that these facilities should be identified as rapidly as possible and specialist centres maintained or created. In 1975, 142 colleges of education in Great Britain trained music specialists. Two of them, Trent Park and Bretton Hall, each had over 100 music students; a further 13 had between 50 and 100 students; and 127 had less than 50 music stu-

dents each. Our calculations suggest that for the future only 5 to 10 specialist music centres will be needed for the 1600 students (amounting to some 400 a year). Care should be taken, when selecting the colleges of higher education to be so designated, that musical excellence and geographical spread are equally taken into account. The preponderance of such institutions in London and the South-East may mean that some excellent institutions are not designated.

181. In addition to these designated institutions providing a course leading to a B.Ed. in music, divided at the end of the second year by the Diploma of Higher Education, there is a need for a university Post-Graduate Course in Education designed for musicians. The University of London Institute of Education runs such a course (together with higher qualifications at Master's and Ph.D. level); so, too, does Reading University. In our view it is doubtful whether there is a need for further courses.

182. Next, there are universities which give joint music and education degrees. These seem to us to be worthwhile and should be encouraged. They resemble, in structure and spirit, the new qualifications being given by the polytechnics, institutes of higher education and technical colleges which have largely superseded the former mixture of colleges of education and technical colleges. Music is available in almost all of them for recreation, and as a general cultural activity, and it is also available in some places as a component, major or minor, of the Diploma of Higher Education (the 2-year qualification), or a CNAA degree, or a degree validated by the local university. In the B.Ed. degrees (and the three year certificate courses now being phased out), therefore, music is available as a major or minor option.

183. **Clearly, it is important that in future no class teacher, especially in primary schools, should have been educated in a higher education institution where there is no music.**

Music specialists proper (that is, those who take regular class music lessons, organise school orchestras and bands, and put on concerts), will be those who have 'majored' in music. It is these who must in all circumstances have been appropriately trained, but all other teachers should have been educated in an environment where music is played and enjoyed.

In-service training

184. A great deal of this analysis is applicable to in-service training. In recent years the number of teachers attending courses, full and part-time, has grown considerably and it is part of the scheme proposed by the James Committee, and accepted in general (though not in detail) by the government and the local authorities, that in-service training should be part of the normal career pattern of every teacher. **In our view the position of both class and instrumental music teaching is such that it is essential that the major commitment of the musical education of teachers should be to in-service training. This in-service training should be of three broad kinds:**

i) Organised by the LEA for general class teachers, and making use of music advisers, outstanding music teachers in schools, peripatetic teachers, private teachers, part-time teachers from local orchestras and music colleges, lecturers in higher education institutes and HMIs.

ii) Initiated by LEAs for their music teachers, but on a longer time-scale and probably with residential elements – e.g. vacation schools organised in co-operation with music colleges, colleges of higher education, music departments of universities, lecturers or performers of distinction.

iii) One term and one year secondment for instrumental teachers to specialist courses at colleges and universities; national courses run by colleges and university departments.

185. The local courses should mainly be directed towards helping the teacher maintain or improve his musical skill. They should be related to the teacher's particular school, the place of music in the general curriculum and the maintenance of teaching skills. There can be no doubt that, if we are to improve the quality of music teaching in the schools in the future, we must find ways of connecting the professional performer and the music academic with this network which will be organised for the most part by the LEA music advisory staff. Wherever possible, in-service training for music specialists should be based upon the institutes that have been designated as specialist music centres.

186. Finally, it is essential that music teachers should be trained to recognise children of exceptional talent and that they should know whom to contact as soon as possible for immediate steps to be taken to give the children the musical training they need. The temptation to keep

a talented child to yourself is strong – there is a delight in discovering and nurturing talent, the child can make a valued contribution to the school, it is wonderful to see a true gift emerging – but the child's own interests must come first. We should remember, too, that a music teacher creates an environment where music is enjoyed and loved. People learn to sing and play; they also become the audiences of the future. All this requires great pedagogic and human qualities. They are specially tested since it is rare for a music teacher to rise to the highest grades of the teaching profession, and he or she sees people of no greater ability, and making less contribution to the life of the community, becoming head teachers. There is little, however, that can be recommended by a committee such as this; it can only be hoped that the importance of the role that the music teacher performs will increasingly be recognised.

Chapter 6
Advanced studies

The need for further provision
Orchestral instrumentalists

187. The Committee has heard much evidence on the gap between the standard reached by the majority of music students at the end of a performer's course at a music college and the requirements of the profession. The extension of all performers' courses to four years is likely to narrow this gap but will not close it. In our view, developments are taking place which suggest that musicians are determined to close the gap. We support the initiatives that have this as their aim, whether now under way or planned, which we describe in this chapter.

188. In the past, those leaving music colleges and aiming at an orchestral career were able to gain valuable experience by working, often seasonally, in one of the many seaside, municipal or spa orchestras; in addition there were opportunities to 'learn the hard way' in cinemas and restaurants. Those opportunities have almost entirely disappeared and it is sometimes argued that they have not been replaced, thus leaving a gap in experience between the requirements of the principal professional orchestras and ensembles on the one hand, and the large body of amateur and semi-professional music making on the other. This situation is in contrast to that existing in Germany, for example, where there are many second tier orchestras in which young professionals can cut their teeth and learn what it is to make one's living as a professional performer in front of audiences whose expectations are not the highest. It can be argued, however, that there are indeed orchestras which in the present organisation of British orchestral music play a role equivalent to that of the pier and spa orchestras of the past. British orchestras really fall into four groups: the four self-managed London orchestras and the BBC Symphony Orchestra; contracted orchestras (including the BBC's) outside London; permanent orchestras of the principal opera companies; and touring accompanying orchestras for opera and ballet. It has been put to us that some of these orchestras could play a role in bridging the gap between the music colleges and the front-rank orchestras

by providing young professionals with the kind of experience that they badly need at the start of their careers.

189. If these orchestras, and the bodies that subsidise them, were prepared to recognise that this is a role that they are already to some extent performing, then a training element could more consciously be built into their public performance function. They would need to allow for more rehearsal time and they would need to be able to attract conductors experienced in orchestral training. But if funds could be found to make this possible, then it would not only be the young professionals who would benefit; the standard of performance of the orchestras themselves could be raised considerably in the process. Mrs Thatcher, when she was Secretary of State for Education, said, in response to a report by the ABO, that it is up to employers to carry out that sort of training which goes beyond what can be expected of the educational system. As other Reports, like 'Going on the Stage', have argued, in the arts there is not the same availability of funds for training as in industry and commerce; it is unrealistic to expect orchestras and opera companies, whose subsidies are inadequate to meet all the demands of the public for their performances, to spend the percentage of their budget on 'in-service training' which would be considered normal in industry or commerce. **We therefore recommend that a working party be established under an independent chairman with representatives from the ABO, the colleges of music, the Musicians' Union, the ISM, the BBC and the Government to examine proposals for a national training scheme along these lines. It is possible that the Arts Council and the Government might participate in the finance of such a scheme by re-allocation of existing funds rather than provision of any substantial new grants. The orchestras concerned might accept specific subsidy to carry out this training work. It has been put to us that some of this work should be organised in such a way as to attract support from the Training Services Agency.**

190. We have dealt with the gap in experience between the end of a college course and acceptance into a major orchestra, but we have also received evidence that at an earlier stage there is need for improvement in the quantity and quality of orchestral training and experience for students during their time at the music colleges. Most colleges are unable to provide within their own resources satisfactory orchestral training and experience with the best sectional coaches and conductors.

It has been argued that there is a need for one or more specialist centres to which some students could be attached for periods of concentrated orchestral training. We have had quoted to us the analogy of a student reading modern languages at a university who is sent abroad for a year as part of his degree course, the expenses being covered by his grant and fee.

191. It has been suggested to us that since orchestras find themselves from time to time tempted to offer engagements to highly talented students who have completed only part of their college courses, an attempt should be made to establish more formal links between the colleges and the orchestras in the way that applies in Berlin between the Karajan Orchestral Academy and the Berlin Philharmonic Orchestra. This Academy accepts thirty students after audition by the Berlin Philharmonic Orchestra and they are then taught by members of the orchestra or of the Academy themselves; they also have regular opportunities to play as deputies in the orchestra. It has been argued that an adaptation of this scheme in Britain could be made on the basis of apprenticeships offered by the major orchestras to those leaving colleges. We can see that this suggestion has merit but we appreciate the doubts expressed both by the ABO and the MU, if only because we can see the difficulties of players 'learning on the job' in orchestras of the first rank where the audience expects the highest possible standard of performance.

192. **It is for this reason that we would prefer to see this particular need met by an extension of the music college course and we therefore welcome the decision of the Royal Northern College of Music to establish in Manchester, possibly with the help of the BBC, a centre for advanced studies where post-graduate, or post-graduate equivalent, students could be offered demanding courses designed to provide a pre-professional training and calculated to enable those successfully completing such courses to enter an orchestra or opera company equipped to make a strong contribution to the work of the company from the outset. We understand that the proposed centre would cater for a 68 piece orchestra, 20 singers, and various pianists and conductors. We also understand that there is a possibility that a post-diploma training scheme for orchestral players may be established in London at Goldsmiths' College as a result of talks now taking place between representatives of the BBC, the Musicians' Union, the ABO, the Arts Council**

and certain educational interests. We think a proposal along these lines is worthy of support.

Other musicians

193. So far we have dealt only with potential orchestral players, mainly because the problem there has seemed intractable in the past. Other students (soloists, composers, conductors and singers), may be able to obtain a grant from a charity or foundation to enable them to study either at a conservatoire abroad or as the pupil of a distinguished musician. For students of outstanding talent an experience of this kind is obviously of value. **Unfortunately the numbers who can obtain funds to take advantage of such advanced study are small and we think it must be a first objective of any new proposals for advanced studies in this country that they should make available to larger numbers of students the benefits of advanced study in the United Kingdom and abroad at the highest level.** This is a field where European co-operation could be of some significance but it is also a realm for private beneficence. However, as things are at the moment, most young performers are likely to seek work at a stage of their development when they still have much more to do to perfect their technique.

194. All these various options, together with training orchestras and summer schools which we discuss later, are in marked contrast to the well ordered progress that a student can make through his training career, on and into the profession in some other European countries. In East Germany, for example, orchestral musicians are generally trained for a period of four or more years. In the case of exceptionally outstanding students, and this particularly applies to wind players, the fourth year can be carried out extra-murally. The student is then also permitted to establish himself in an orchestra. Contracts between the colleges of music and local symphony and opera orchestras stipulate that advanced students can participate as musicians in the orchestra or take over the part of an instrumental soloist, singer or conductor. Contractual stipulations also provide for a delegation of instrumentalists from the Leipzig College of Music to work as deputies in the Gewandhaus Orchestra, in the municipal theatre of Leipzig, or in the Halle Philharmonic. Other colleges of music in East Germany formulate similar training programmes in co-operation with local orchestras. The results of the East German highly-disciplined approach have been strikingly demonstrated by their achievements in other fields, such as

sport. Although we live in a very different kind of society, we would do well to try and match some of their dedication.

Post-graduate training orchestras
The former Academy of the BBC

195. The Academy of the BBC, originally the New BBC Orchestra and intermediately the BBC Training Orchestra, was formed in January 1966 'to provide intensive orchestral experience immediately following an instrumentalist's course at a school of music'. It originally had a strength of between 65 and 70 players and these were engaged on a contract which might last for one (minimum), two, or three (maximum) years. From the start the Orchestra broadcast once a week from the studio and it played in public once a month. It was salaried at a level originally very close to the fully professional rank-and-file contract rate, but latterly substantially less. It was never the BBC's intention that the musicians leaving the Orchestra would be contracted exclusively to BBC orchestras and, over the years, only about a quarter of them have joined BBC orchestras on leaving. In January 1972 the BBC felt obliged to reduce the size of the Orchestra to 35. This reduction saved the BBC about £50,000 a year. The BBC also reserved the right to review the situation in 1977. Early in 1974 the BBC began again to consider the future of the orchestra, consulting – informally – both the Arts Council and the DES. In March 1975, the Musicians' Union was informed, officially, of the BBC's regret that, after September 1977, it could not continue to administer and finance, without support from the musical profession, what it felt should be a 'national training orchestra'. The ABO was given the same information in December 1975. The Academy was in fact wound up in June 1977, when it became no longer viable. **If the proposed centre for advanced studies at Manchester with its 68 piece orchestra and the proposed post-diploma training scheme for orchestral players in London (referred to in the previous section) both come to fruition, then the vacuum left by the demise of the Academy will have been satisfactorily filled.**

Snape Maltings Training Orchestra
196. Founded in 1975, the Snape Maltings Training Orchestra was originally composed of young string players who were drawn to the string master classes held at the Maltings, and was formed to give continuity to the teaching. The orchestra now consists of twenty-four string players who assemble for three one-week courses in the year

under the Director of String Studies of the Britten-Pears School, Cecil Aronowitz. No fees are charged for the periodic courses which generally extend over a period of two years. A small group of wind players joins the strings where required. The orchestra has appeared at the Aldeburgh Festival, St John's Smith Square and other arts centres, and other outside engagements are planned. Admission is by audition and the standard of playing required is high.

The Rehearsal Orchestra

197. The Rehearsal Orchestra runs residential courses in Edinburgh (during the Festival) and London (during the Prom season) and other week-end courses elsewhere in the country. The courses are open to students, teachers, amateurs and young professionals. It seeks to expand players' knowledge and experience of orchestral playing under professional conditions. It aims at complementing the work of the music colleges and is especially useful for aspiring orchestral players who lack training in orchestral style and technique. It also provides opportunities for young professional soloists (instrumentalists and singers) to work with a full symphony orchestra, and for composers to hear a run-through of a new work for the first time. It has held one week-end course per annum in conjunction with the London Opera Centre. Equally important are opportunities it provides to players outside London by holding courses in various regional centres. We believe that the role of the Rehearsal Orchestra is important and deserving of support.

A Comparison from Overseas – The National Training Orchestra of Australia

198. With the various proposals that are now developing in the UK for advanced orchestral training, we felt that it would be useful to include an example of a successful scheme that operates in Australia. The scheme, which is run by the Australian Broadcasting Corporation first aimed to train young qualified musicians in orchestral techniques and repertoire, and secondly to form a pool of players which would provide a steady stream of experienced musicians of the standard required by Australia's leading orchestras. The scheme provides for 32 players each with A$4000 a year scholarship with a further allowance of A$500 a year for those players required to live away from home. Scholarships for string players are for two years while all other sections are for one year. In each case, there is provision for players to continue their studies for an extra year. The programme of training is in a wide

range of repertoire from baroque to contemporary, including Australian compositions. The annual intake is about 16 players; the players are engaged full-time and the schedule of work is 30 hours per week, which includes 6 hours private practice. Tutorials are conducted by leading musicians and solo performances take place with other members of the orchestra as an audience. The average number of public performances is approximately 12 a year.

Schools of advanced studies and occasional courses
The Britten-Pears School for Advanced Musical Studies
199. The long-term education aim of the Aldeburgh Festival-Snape Maltings Foundation is to create at Snape a full-time, nationally recognised music school of a unique character. The Britten-Pears School for Advanced Musical Studies will concentrate in the first instance on advanced studies in three areas. The School, it must be emphasized, will not offer general courses for students of average ability and thus duplicate work that is done elsewhere. The accent at Snape will be on exceptional standards of excellence and advanced ability. The first area of study will comprise courses for singers, under the Director of Singing, Peter Pears; the second, courses for string players, under the Director of Strings, Cecil Aronowitz. In both areas it is the firm intent to offer intensive, advanced training and coaching to small groups of singers and players whose technical attainments and potential musicality are of a sufficiently advanced standard to qualify them to undertake the courses. The third area, theoretical studies under Donald Mitchell, will include a wide variety of subjects such as history, composition, style, analysis and oriental music, and special intensive studies of composers and particular musical territories historically associated with Aldeburgh, with the Festival and the work of its founding Artistic Directors.

International Musicians' Seminar, Prussia Cove
200. The IMS Seminar at Prussia Cove near Penzance is in its seventh year and takes place annually for 3 weeks in the spring. The Seminar, which was originally the inspiration of Sandor Vegh and Hilary Behrens, caters for up to 60 advanced players between 16 and 30 who have experience as soloists, and for quartets and ensembles that have been working together over a period. The principle on which the seminars are based is that, at the highest level of training for young professionals, there is no substitute for master classes. The professors, who in recent

years have included Bruno Giuranna, Paul Szabo and Radu Aldulescu in addition to Sandor Vegh, also play with those attending the Seminar in a series of concerts, both in public and informally in the evenings. A large proportion of the performers who attend come from Europe and America and, in that respect, the Seminars are a reversal of the traditional process whereby young British performers go abroad to perfect their talents. In 1977 the IMS was expanded to include 10 days of open chamber music, based on the ideas that have been developed at Marlboro in the United States by Rudolph Serkin and the Busch Quartet. About 40 musicians took part, roughly half of them being those who had taken part in the 3 week course and the rest being established performers joining the Seminar for the 10 days of open chamber music. During this period each musician is scheduled to play in several different groupings and combinations, the purpose being to allow musicians of different ages and experience to interact with each other on a basis of equality and to explore music of all periods without limitation of rehearsal time. There are plans to extend this period of open chamber music to three weeks in 1978.

Dartington Summer School
201. In a different category, in that it does not solely cater for the advanced student of a high standard, is the Dartington Summer School which welcomes every kind of music lover, including the ordinary listener. Most of the programme is taken up by concerts, lectures and choral singing, but there are also smaller classes for professional musicians, teachers and students, as well as classes of general interest. Open master classes are held, but those who perform in them are specially selected. The Summer School lasts for 4 weeks from late July to late August, but each week is self-contained so that those attending can book for one, two, three weeks or for the whole course.

A standing conference for advanced music studies
202. We believe that the opportunities for orchestral training and advanced studies that we have detailed in this chapter perform a vital function for young performers by making it possible for them to raise their playing to the highest standards. We recommend that every effort should be made to enable all of them to flourish and to cater for a larger number of performers. If they are to do this effectively their efforts need to be co-ordinated. We believe that there is scope for a Standing Conference for Advanced Music

Studies, whose job it would be to co-ordinate, on an advisory basis, the organisation of the studies detailed in this chapter, as well as occasional courses that exist elsewhere in the UK. An important part of the role of such a Standing Conference should be to raise funds from public sources, private charities and trusts, and from industry and commerce, to enable these enterprises in the field of advanced studies to be placed on a secure financial basis.

203. It may well be, too, that a National Council for Music Training, representing the training institutions, the Musicians' Union, other professional bodies and employers' organisations should be established, along the lines of the National Council for Drama Training, in order to review the evolving circumstances of training for music. The parties involved should give serious consideration to this suggestion.

Starting a career

204. We received a considerable amount of evidence to the effect that there is a great need for more advice and guidance to be available to young professionals at the start of their career. Many students, whose musical talents have been developed to a high standard, have little idea how to put those talents to practical use and earn a living from them. The young professional needs to know how to assemble the various publicity material he or she will need – photographs, biographical details, press cuttings, brochures and the like; whether to give a London debut recital; how to approach agents, municipal entertainment officers, music clubs and societies, music festivals, regional arts associations, schools, universities, recording companies, radio and television, indeed the whole range of possible opportunities for engagements; and not least how to cope with insurance, VAT and income tax, and what help to expect from bank managers, solicitors, insurance brokers and accountants, all of whom will be needed at some time or other.

205. At the present time various attempts (largely unco-ordinated) are being made to help the young professional at the start of his or her career. Various fellowships and bursaries are offered by organisations such as the Calouste Gulbenkian Foundation and the Leverhulme, Martin and Countess of Munster Trusts. Each year the National Federation of Music Societies offer an award to young concert artists. The award consists of a small cash prize, at least ten engagements with

member societies, a small sum of money to enable the winner to commission a new work and a recital at the Wigmore Hall. The award is in a five-yearly cycle for men's voices, pianists, string players, ladies' voices and wind players. Very many young artists have been given their first opportunities on the concert platform by NFMS societies. The Federation encourages societies to promote one concert a year at which young artists can make their first appearance. Its member societies promote some 3,000 concerts per year; this gives great opportunity for these young artists. The Ralph Vaughan Williams Trust is placing an increasing emphasis on helping young performers at their point of entry into the profession. The Young Artists Recitals promoted by the regional arts associations, the Park Lane Group and the ISM also provide valuable opportunities to soloists and ensembles.

206. Among initiatives taken by individuals in recent years to help the young professional, there is Yehudi Menuhin's scheme 'Live Music Now', which has yet to prove itself; the subscription recitals by young artists which Peter Katin has been running as a private venture in his own studio; and the seminars given by Leonard Pearcey. As far as artists' agents are concerned, the present situation is that the smaller and more exclusive agents are, quite fairly from their point of view, inclined to concentrate on a limited number of artists to whom they can guarantee a high degree of personal attention, and they are naturally unable by that very criterion to take on very many. The larger agents may put people on their books, but this all too often means a lack of the very attention that a young artist so badly needs, apart from which they frequently take the view that the artist should get dates for himself before coming to them. It has been put to us that there is a need for an independent, non-profit, concert agency to help young professionals at the start of their careers for a period of not more than five years from the date at which they complete their full-time studies. After the five year period, or sooner if they wished, the young professionals would move on to commercial management. The agency would be concerned not only with obtaining bookings, but also with the whole business of training in career management. We believe this proposal is worth further constructive thought.

207. The future of music in this country must rest on the development of first-rate talent early enough in a young career. There is at the moment very little follow-through from the education and training of a

young musician to his or her guidance through the difficult early stages of a professional career. It is crucial that young musicians have the best opportunities to perform early enough for their potential to be judged. It is equally important that they themselves discover at an early stage whether they have the physical and emotional stamina to sustain a performing career as a professional musician.

Chapter 7
Summary of conclusions and recommendations

Training the school-age musician

1. At primary level, the first priority is for musically gifted and talented children to be properly identified and encouraged. Local education authority (LEA) advisers should draw up guidelines that will help to alert primary school heads and their staff to what may be real musical talent in a child. Much can be learnt about the nature of giftedness and talent, and how to deal with it, from experience in other areas including non-academic areas such as sport. (paras 35-42)

2. Much of the training of gifted and talented children will take place outside the school. LEAs should be prepared to subsidise private lessons more widely that they do at present. In particular, they should draw up panels of local instrumental teachers whom they consider suitable to teach in Saturday and evening music centres and to give private lessons out of school hours to pupils sponsored by LEAs.

(paras 54-55)

3. Promotion prospects for music specialist teachers in primary schools should be improved, with more opportunity to rise to posts on higher salary scales. Music specialists and music advisory teachers should be encouraged to show their non-specialist colleagues how to handle musical experiences with children that can be within the competence of those without musical training. Among these experiences, BBC schools broadcasts and traditional class singing are particularly important. Primary schools should nominate one class teacher to be responsible for liaison with visiting instrumental teachers so that a child's instrumental training can be more closely integrated with the rest of his or her education.

(paras 43-52)

4. At secondary level, LEAs should be as flexible as possible in the arrangements they make for providing musical training, relating their provision as far as possible both to the circumstances of their area and the specific needs of each individual pupil. They should be prepared to

support their gifted children at the specialist music schools. The financial commitment will be slight, since such children are rare. In some areas of the country, notably the larger conurbations, LEAs should consider establishing a specialist music wing along the lines of the Pimlico model in one of their comprehensive schools, but care should be taken that this is not done in an area where it would duplicate the role of one of the existing specialist music schools.   (paras 56-67)

5. For talented children in ordinary secondary schools the most important need is to improve the quality of instrumental training available to them. This training is usually provided by peripatetic teachers during school hours or at LEA evening or weekend music centres. The number of such centres, whether sited in purpose-built premises or involving the ad hoc use of school buildings during out-of-school hours, has greatly increased since the publication of *Making Musicians* in 1965. There is room for further expansion. An important advantage of basing music training on music centres is that use can be made of instrumental teachers who are themselves professional performers, but who would usually be unable to teach regularly in schools since they are not qualified as class teachers. These professional musicians represent an invaluable reservoir of experience and technical accomplishment, and LEAs should make maximum use of those available in their area.

(paras 68-76)

6. A major difficulty for the young musician during the years spent preparing for 'O' and 'A' level examinations are the competing claims of academic work and practice time on the instrument. Pressures to take a prescribed number of subjects at 'O' and 'A' level can seriously interfere with musical training. The fact that the University of London Examinations Council is introducing a new 'A' level scheme in 1980, comprising separate practical, theoretical and combined practice and theory examinations is greatly to be welcomed. Double 'O' and 'A' levels in performance and theory should be legitimate options in music and candidates should be able to take either or both. There should also be more opportunities for the 16-19 age group to take specialist courses in music at schools, colleges of further education or 6th form colleges.

(paras 80-85)

7. In some parts of the country the young musician faces serious difficulties on account of the uneven spread of provision for a musical

training between different LEAs. The local authority associations should encourage their members to improve the provision in those parts of the country where it is inadequate.   (para 86)

The specialist music schools

8. Gifted children need the stimulus and company of other gifted children. They also need regular and frequent access to teachers who understand their gift and can help them. Between them, the five existing specialist schools represent a variety of different approaches to the training of the gifted young musician. The need is not to provide more of them, but to achieve financial security for those that already exist and to enable the small number of gifted children who satisfy the entrance requirements to attend one or other of the specialist music schools, from whatever part of the country they may come. The five schools should therefore either become direct grant schools or be maintained by local authorities with expenditure on 'out-county' pupils recovered as it is for special schools for other purposes.   (paras 87-96)

9. In addition to the specialist music schools, the choir schools play an important part in training musicians. The education they provide is of great value and LEAs should contribute to the fees of children awarded choral scholarships.   (paras 97-98)

The music colleges

10. All music colleges should offer four year first degree courses in order to raise the standard of achievement attained by students at the end of their course. The first two years should be a basic course normally leading to a Diploma of Higher Education. Students admitted to this course should qualify for a mandatory grant. The second two years would lead to a degree, or degree equivalent qualification, and should also qualify the student for a mandatory grant. Special arrangements should be made to ensure that the gifted musician without two 'A' levels or equivalent qualification is not denied a grant.

(paras 103-124)

11. The music colleges should concentrate mainly on the training of intending performers and instrumental teachers rather than on those seeking a higher education in music or intending primarily to become teachers. This will mean a reduction in the number of students entering the music colleges, but the fact that all music colleges will be offering

four year courses will mean that the number of students at the music colleges at any one time will be only slightly less than at present. In order to improve the quality of instrumental teaching available to children in future years, instruction in how to teach the instrument should be an important part of most music college courses.

(paras 103-124)

12. Those students who wish to obtain a qualification as a class teacher specialising in music (of whom only a small number will be required in future on account of the decline in the child population) should have several options open to them. If they want to go to a music college, they could go for two years only, take the Dip. H.E. and then go on to a college of higher education offering music as a major option in order to obtain a B.Ed. degree, or they could take a B.Ed. at one of these colleges of higher education and not go to music college at all. Others will go to a university. Alternatively, if they wish to raise the standard of their performance to a high level, then they should be able to choose between one specially designated music college that offers a four year instrumental teacher's course with a class teaching qualification built into the course, concurrently with instrumental training, *or* one college of higher education similarly designated for this purpose and with its staff and facilities suitably developed. (paras 109-124)

13. In addition to raising standards, the principal advantage of the four year music college course outlined above is the flexibility that it offers. Students can choose to spend four years or two years at music college. If they spend only two years, then they can either go on to a college of higher education to obtain qualified teacher status, or go on to a university, or in very rare cases they may even go straight into the profession before completing the course. Conversely, it would be possible in certain cases for those who start at a university or college of higher education to transfer to music college for their final two years. (para 123)

14. The music colleges in London face particular difficulties at the present time on account of the fact that, unlike most of the other music colleges, they are not part of the public sector. It is unsatisfactory in principle that the form of public subsidy provided to some of the most eminent colleges in the country should be one of a guarantee against loss rather than a positive programme for the development of music training and education. (paras 156-159)

15. In any discussion of the way the London colleges are organised it is necessary to separate the Guildhall School of Music and the London College of Music from the three colleges at present in receipt of direct subsidy from the DES – the Royal Academy, the Royal College and Trinity College. The Guildhall receives a revenue subsidy from the Corporation of the City of London; it is now housed in a new complex in the Barbican; it is combined with a drama school; and, as well as running full-time courses, it also caters for a large number of part-time students. However, the school now faces a serious financial crisis on account of the high cost of running the new building. A further subsidy is needed in addition to that provided by the City. It could well be that the School should link itself with the City of London Polytechnic or City University in order to provide itself with a suitable basis for public subsidy.   (paras 156-159)

16. The Royal Academy of Music, the Royal College of Music and Trinity College of Music should either become monotechnics maintained by local authorities or they should become colleges of London University. In view of its experience in training instrumental teachers, Trinity should be linked with an existing teacher training institution and should be the one music college that offers a four year course with a teaching qualification built in as part of the course.   (paras 156-159)

17. The nature of music training requires a higher level of individual instruction than that needed in most other areas of higher education. The student teacher ratio should be of the same order as that existing in medical schools, namely 5 : 1, rather than the 8½ : 1 that normally exists in higher education.   (paras 125-128)

18. Orchestral playing should be given a high priority within music college courses in terms of the time allotted to it. The music colleges should use their resources to make the fullest use of good coaches and conductors. In particular, there should be more opportunities for students from the London colleges to take part in joint ventures.

(paras 129-133)

19. In the case of singers, LEAs should be prepared to defer or extend grants until a singer's voice has matured sufficiently to take advantage of the rigorous training necessary. In places where there are opera companies, students should be able to gain in-service training through

periods of secondment to these companies. The proposal for a National Opera Studio to take the place of the London Opera Centre is one that we support. (paras 134-137)

20. For the young composer, the greatest need is that he should be able to hear his music performed as he develops. The Arts Council of Great Britain should consider providing more funds for the preparation and playing of new music by promising young composers as soon as they emerge from full-time study. (paras 138-141)

21. Similarly, funds should be made available to enable the opera houses to maintain one or two young conductors in addition to their normal establishment. Student conductors should be given favourable consideration when they apply for postgraduate awards, since they may have necessarily exhausted their grant entitlement in training to become a good enough musician to go on to study as a conductor.

(paras 142-144)

22. Students at the music colleges in London face particular difficulties on account of lack of residential accommodation near their colleges and the consequent need to spend much time and money on travelling to and from their colleges. The present total provision of about 200 residential places should be trebled. An immediate attempt should be made to house an additional 400 students within easy access of their colleges by making use of surplus accommodation becoming available from the closure of colleges of education or other public buildings that would be unsuitable for normal family accommodation. All music colleges should offer more career advice, especially in relation to the period at the end of full-time study when students are trying to establish themselves in the profession. (paras 101 and 151-155)

23. Under present arrangements teaching staff at music colleges in London are not remunerated on a scale comparable with other higher education establishments and do not have comparable conditions of employment. Fees should be raised by placing them on a pro-rata basis, linked to full-time salaries for comparable posts in higher education. Conditions of service and relationships between staff, principals and governing bodies should be brought into line with those prevailing in other higher education establishments in the public sector.

(paras 146-150)

University departments of music

24. Applications to read music at universities are likely to increase in view of the severe contraction of music courses in initial teacher training. Universities should develop links with other bodies such as polytechnics, colleges of higher education and the regional arts associations in order to make the best use of their resources. For performers who emerge from university music departments the normal form of postgraduate study should be at a music college. In cities where university music departments and music colleges exist together, flexible courses should be developed to give individual students the best balance possible in their musical education. (paras 160-171)

Institutions for training class music teachers

25. Apart from the four year course at Trinity College of Music, future class music teachers should be drawn from a limited number of institutions with a strong commitment to music. Five to ten colleges of higher education should be so designated on the basis of musical excellence and location. University postgraduate courses in education designed for musicians should perhaps be available only at London and Reading. In view of the sharp reduction in the number of teachers being trained, there should be a major commitment to the provision of in-service music training for existing teachers. (paras 172-186)

Advanced studies

26. In order to improve the standard of orchestral playing achieved by young musicians applying to join one of the major orchestras, a working party should be set up to consider the extent to which certain touring and accompanying orchestras can fulfil a training role. Particular attention should be paid to the possibility of organising this work in such a way that it will attract subsidy from the Training Services Agency. (paras 187-189)

27. Current initiatives to develop advanced studies, including those at the Royal Northern College of Music in Manchester and at Goldsmiths' College in London, should be supported by the authorities concerned. (para 192)

28. In the field of advanced studies the aim should be to make available to a larger number of students the benefits of advanced study in the United Kingdom at the highest level. Various schools of advanced studies

(such as the Britten-Pears School for Advanced Musical Studies), occasional schools and seminars (such as the International Musicians' Seminar at Prussia Cove) and training orchestras seek to meet this need in their different ways. A Standing Conference for Advanced Music Studies should be set up to help co-ordinate and expand such activities and, in particular, to raise funds from charities and trusts and industry and commerce, in order to support them. There is also a need for an independent, non-profit, concert agency to help young musicians at the start of their careers. (paras 199-207)

29. The Government Statistical Service should carry out a thorough study of employment in the artistic professions. (para 100)

Appendix A

List of individuals and organisations that submitted written or oral evidence to the Enquiry, gave information, or were consulted

Paul Abbott
Ruth Abel
Hilary Alcock
Philomena Alston
D. M. Annett
John Armstrong
Richard Armstrong
Professor Denis Arnold
Cecil Aronowitz
Arts Council of Great Britain
Associated Board of the Royal
  Schools of Music
Association of British
  Orchestras
Australian Broadcasting
  Commission

R. Barrett-Ayres
Dr Kenneth Barritt
Kenneth van Barthold
Dr Jean Battersby
Charles Beardsall
Hilary Behrens
Peter Bellingham
Atarah Ben-Tovim
Wallace Berry
John Bingham
Wendy Bird
Birmingham School of Music
M. Blee
Kathleen Blocksidge

Roy Bohana
Lord Boyle
Anthony Bramall
British Actors' Equity
  Association
British Broadcasting
  Corporation
British Federation of Brass
  Bands
British Federation of Music
  Festivals
Roderick Brydon
M. A. E. Burton
Edward D. Butler

Mary Cadogan
Alwyn Calvert
Cambridgeshire College of Arts
  & Technology
A. B. Cameron
Ida Carroll
Louis Carus
Chetham School of Music
Beryl Chempin
Chester College
George Christie
Marta Clare
Clarendon College
Eta Cohen
Colchester Institute of Higher
  Education

Conservatoire National
  Supérieur de Musique, Paris
B. W. N. Cooper
Imogen Cooper
Zoe Cooper
County of Avon
Peter Cox
Philip Cranmer
John Cruft
John G. Cullen

Martin Dalby
Kathleen Dale
Dartington College of Arts
Professor Cedric Thorpe Davie
Dept. of Education & Science
Brian Dickie
Joan Dickson
Christie Duncan

Brian Eastop
Educational Institute of Scotland
Raymond Edwards
Reynold Elder
Jack Elliott
European String Teachers
  Association
Ken M. Evans
Professor Peter Evans

Andrew N. Fairbairn
Horace Fitzpatrick
Myers Foggin
Dr Richard Fong
Patrick Forbes
L. Friedman

Professor Edward Garden
Michael Garrick
Ruth Gipps

Sir Alexander Gibson
Stanley Glasser
Sir William Glock
Professor Alexander Goehr
Peter Graeme
Keith Grant
John Graty
Laurence Gray
B. J. Griffiths
Eric Griffiths
Guild for the Promotion of
  Welsh Music
Guildhall School of Music and
  Drama

The Earl of Harewood
Simon Harris
Peter Theodore Harrison
Sidney Harrison
Kato Havas
Norman Hearn
Peter Hemmings
Stan Hibbert
Mary Hill
Hochschule der Künste, Berlin
Hannah Horovitz
Keith Howard
W. N. J. Howard
Huddersfield School of Music
Dr Donald Hughes
Ieuan Hughes
Wallis Hunt
George Hurst

Incorporated Society of
  Musicians
Peter Isherwood

Nannie Jamieson
Walter Jeffrey
Glynne Jones

Kenneth V. Jones
Juilliard School, New York

Peter Katin
Michael Kaye
Bernard Keeffe
Ivor Keys

Brian Lane
Leeds College of Music
Ronald Lees
Nicola LeFanu
Harry Legge
Lawrence Leonard
Sir Anthony Lewis
Arnold Lewis
Dilys E. Lewis
Live Music Now
Dr W. S. Lloyd Webber
London Chanticleer Orchestra
& London Repertoire
Orchestra
London College of Music

Mannes School of Music,
New York
Peter Marcan
Sheila Marshall
Robert H. Masters
Professor William Mathias
Sir Robert Mayer
J. McAdam
Denis McCaldin
Gerald McDonald
Richard McNicol
Professor Wilfrid Mellers
Yehudi Menuhin School
Middlesex Polytechnic
A. Millar
Ministère des Affaires
Culturelles, Paris

Kathleen Mitchell
Ernest Mongor
Rex Montgomery
Philip Moore
Roland Morris
John Morton
Peter Mountain
James Mowat
Simon Murphy
Musicians' Union
Music Advisers' National
Association

National Association for Gifted
Children
National Association of Music
Students' Unions
National Federation of Music
Societies

Sheila Oakes
Professor Robin Orr

Robin Page
Manoug Parikian
W. H. Parry
Dr John Paynter
Leonard Pearcey
Allen Percival
Jill Phillips
Pimlico School
James Porter
J. Maxwell Pryce
Leonard Pugh
Purcell School

Alan Quilter

Ralph Vaughan Williams Trust
Rehearsal Orchestra

Peter Renshaw
Lenore Reynell
David Richardson
Richmond Orchestra
Frederick Riddle
Professor Frederick Rimmer
Anthony Rooley
Royal Academy of Music
Royal Academy of Music
  Teaching Staff Association
Royal College of Music
Royal Northern College of
  Music
Royal Scottish Academy of
  Music and Drama
Rural Music Schools Assocn.

Dr Helmut Schulze
Scottish Arts Council
Scottish Education Department
M. Sheldon
Bernard Shore
James Sloggie
Professor Basil Smallman
Clive Smart
Janet Smith
Rodney Smith
Ronald Smith
Roderick Spencer
Pamela Spofforth
David Squibb
St Mary's Music School
St Paul's Girls School
St Paul's Preparatory School
Standing Conference of
  Amateur Music
Stannington College of Further
  Education
David A. Stevenson
Jack Stoddart

Strathclyde Regional Council
Dr W. H. Swinburne
L. Sykes

Dorothy Taylor
Dr William Taylor
Rev. Duncan Thomson
Professor Michael Tilmouth
Michael Toll
David Toplis
Dennis Townhill
Trinity College of Music
Professor Brian Trowell

University Grants Committee

John Vallins

Alfredo Wang
Dr Ernest Warburton
Eleanor Warren
Professor Raymond Warren
David Waterman
Wells Cathedral School
Moray Welsh
Welsh Arts Council
Welsh College of Music and
  Drama
J. B. Westcombe
William Whittle
An Chang Williams
Tony Wills
Herbert Winterbottom
Audrey Wisbey
Michael Wood
Professor Ronald Woodham
Woolston County High School
Worshipful Company of
  Musicians

Christopher Yates

Appendix B

Candidates examined by the Associated Board of the Royal Schools of Music in 1965 and 1976.

Grade 4

Subject	Pass	Merit	Distinction	Examined
Pianoforte	6,737	2,416	701	11,595
Organ	42	43	21	110
Violin	711	370	106	1,296
Viola	49	25	3	86
Violoncello	116	58	34	240
Double Bass	19	18	5	47
Flute	125	89	30	257
Oboe	35	37	23	98
Clarinet	325	164	46	578
Bassoon	7	6	1	16
Horn	24	5	2	33
Trumpet or Cornet	39	22	9	87
Trombone	17	4	1	23
Other Brass	—	—	—	—
Instruments		2	—	7
Harp	1	1	—	5
Singing	228	128	3	423
Musicianship	71	56	37	176
Theory	2,645	—	31	2,692
Total	**11,195**	**3,444**	**1,053**	**17,769**

Grade 5

Subject	Pass	Merit	Distinction	Examined
Pianoforte	3,839	1,060	325	7,025
Organ	45	56	22	131
Violin	513	333	149	1,085
Viola	47	28	14	95
Violoncello	99	61	48	229
Double Bass	12	19	9	42
Flute	96	93	36	239
Oboe	44	33	20	105
Clarinet	216	132	58	443
Bassoon	10	5	6	23
Horn	23	10	5	42
Trumpet or Cornet	52	30	9	101
Trombone	11	17	1	35
Other Brass	1	1	—	2
Instruments	1	1	—	2
Harp	—	—	—	—
Singing	267	201	64	552
Musicianship	43	24	9	82
Theory	8,249	—	—	8,450
Total	**13,568**	**2,104**	**775**	**18,683**

Grade 6

Subject	Pass	Merit	Distinction	Examined
Pianoforte	2,193	916	289	4,351
Organ	37	55	26	123
Violin	197	158	84	486
Viola	22	17	10	56
Violoncello	64	46	23	155
Double Bass	1	5	2	8
Flute	26	45	21	95
Oboe	26	22	16	67
Clarinet	58	46	28	154
Bassoon	3	4	3	12
Horn	3	7	3	16
Trumpet or Cornet	16	14	4	34
Trombone	12	3	7	25
Other Brass	1	3	—	4
Instruments	—	2	—	2
Harp	—	—	—	—
Singing	150	107	50	325
Musicianship	35	23	8	79
Theory	627	—	—	1,277
Total	**3,471**	**1,473**	**595**	**7,269**
Piano Duets (Junior)	18	21	12	53

Grade 7

Subject	Pass	Merit	Distinction	Examined
Pianoforte	1,285	556	282	2,682
Organ	36	52	21	113
Violin	184	125	70	407
Viola	14	8	1	26
Violoncello	24	34	22	88
Double Bass	3	1	5	10
Singing	99	100	36	248
Musicianship	14	7	7	31
Theory	474	—	103	602
Total	**2,133**	**883**	**547**	**4,207**
Piano Duets (Middle)	6	9	5	22

Grade 8

Subject	Pass	Merit	Distinction	Examined
Pianoforte	690	407	177	1,723
Organ	46	58	36	144
Violin	81	63	62	233
Viola	8	11	13	34
Violoncello	18	22	23	70
Flute	22	28	30	85
Oboe	18	17	14	53
Clarinet	49	32	24	118
Bassoon	2	2	2	8
Horn	—	9	1	11
Trumpet or Cornet	12	14	6	35
Trombone	1	5	5	11
Instruments	—	—	1	1
Singing	104	99	51	285
Theory	301	—	39	407
Total	**1,352**	**767**	**484**	**3,218**
Piano Duets (Senior)	4	6	10	22

20 Singing Classes: 7 Distinction; 10 Merit; 3 Pass.
2 Chamber Music groups: 1 Merit; 1 Pass.

1965

SUBJECT	Grade 3 Examined	Grade 3 Distinction	Grade 3 Merit	Grade 3 Pass	Grade 2 Examined	Grade 2 Distinction	Grade 2 Merit	Grade 2 Pass	Grade 1 Examined	Grade 1 Distinction	Grade 1 Merit	Grade 1 Pass	Total Examined	Total Distinction	Total Merit	Total Pass
Pianoforte...	10,732	690	2,358	6,314	15,381	823	3,287	9,395	19,243	1,632	5,419	11,107	72,732	4,919	16,419	41,560
Organ ...	—	—	—	—	2,100	181	572	1,095	2,188	195	564	1,185	621	126	264	206
Violin ...	1,673	186	458	871	152	14	35	85	288	36	98	138	9,468	1,033	2,643	4,837
Viola ...	127	14	37	69	311	44	97	147	—	—	—	—	576	69	161	294
Violoncello	308	65	99	133	—	—	—	—	—	—	—	—	1,689	295	515	739
Double Bass	—	—	—	—	—	—	—	—	—	—	—	—	107	21	43	35
Flute ...	285	39	91	137	—	—	—	—	—	—	—	—	961	156	346	406
Oboe ...	137	13	40	75	—	—	—	—	—	—	—	—	460	86	149	198
Clarinet ...	736	67	206	407	—	—	—	—	—	—	—	—	2,029	223	580	1,055
Bassoon ...	15	5	4	5	—	—	—	—	—	—	—	—	74	17	21	27
Horn ...	59	4	13	33	—	—	—	—	—	—	—	—	161	15	44	83
Trumpet or Cornet ...	155	18	38	76	—	—	—	—	—	—	—	—	412	46	118	195
Trombone ...	48	2	9	29	—	—	—	—	—	—	—	—	142	16	38	70
Other Brass Instruments	8	2	2	4	—	—	—	—	—	—	—	—	22	3	8	10
Harp ...	7	2	3	1	—	—	—	—	—	—	—	—	16	5	7	3
Singing ...	—	—	—	—	—	—	—	—	—	—	—	—	1,833	238	635	848
Musicianship	—	—	—	—	—	—	—	—	—	—	—	—	368	55	110	163
Theory ...	3,137	—	—	3,018	3,804	—	—	3,620	5,160	—	—	4,805	25,529	737	—	23,739
	17,427	1,107	3,358	11,172	21,748	1,062	3,991	14,342	26,879	1,863	6,081	17,235	117,200	8,060	22,101	74,468
Piano Duets													97	27	36	28
													117,297	8,087	22,137	74,496

16 Candidates were examined for L.R.S.M., in Dublin:

L.R.S.M. General Paper: 17 examined (15 Pass, 2 Fail)

15 in Branch C Teaching: 12 Pianoforte; 1 Violin; 2 Organ (6 Pass, 9 Fail)   1 in Branch D Performing; Pianoforte (Pass)

Appendix B (*cont.*)

SUBJECT	Grade 8 Examined	Grade 8 Distinction	Grade 8 Merit	Grade 8 Pass	Grade 7 Examined	Grade 7 Distinction	Grade 7 Merit	Grade 7 Pass	Grade 6 Examined	Grade 6 Distinction	Grade 6 Merit	Grade 6 Pass	Grade 5 Examined	Grade 5 Distinction	Grade 5 Merit	Grade 5 Pass	Grade 4 Examined	Grade 4 Distinction	Grade 4 Merit	Grade 4 Pass
Pianoforte...	2,927	364	664	1,222	4,228	488	1,056	2,003	5,994	396	1,109	3,044	13,750	913	2,884	7,618	13,473	693	2,481	7,849
Organ ...	141	45	50	38	101	30	41	27	115	25	45	40	136	36	59	33	130	25	62	38
Violin ...	556	168	180	159	1,013	231	292	392	1,077	174	295	485	2,646	306	706	1,268	2,689	259	703	1,447
Viola ...	106	43	29	30	118	30	30	46	158	21	54	64	305	51	91	135	327	37	84	170
Violoncello ...	196	56	76	47	313	83	102	104	446	108	122	182	847	171	251	362	861	138	277	379
Double Bass	24	5	9	9	—	—	—	—	52	6	18	21	100	13	42	36	81	7	23	43
Guitar ...	104	12	33	43	—	—	—	—	113	11	34	53	329	26	78	168	497	29	156	263
Flute ...	508	141	164	166	—	—	—	—	697	125	268	258	1,661	247	457	808	1,859	203	506	962
Oboe ...	249	78	92	67	—	—	—	—	353	85	121	137	669	96	227	288	747	110	273	330
Clarinet ...	595	103	161	245	—	—	—	—	1,080	96	277	516	3,055	227	711	1,716	3,871	212	904	2,399
Bassoon ...	87	27	31	23	—	—	—	—	89	24	25	37	186	39	62	72	152	21	62	64
Horn ...	128	33	36	51	—	—	—	—	144	28	52	54	402	59	102	195	480	40	126	261
Trumpet ...	203	32	67	83	—	—	—	—	255	30	63	126	1,046	74	243	544	1,485	118	387	826
Trombone ...	109	28	41	33	—	—	—	—	160	19	40	85	405	44	103	211	521	45	121	282
Other Brass	123	30	44	36	—	—	—	—	141	22	41	59	750	85	227	352	873	106	242	449
Harp ...	—	—	—	—	8	3	3	1	7	4	1	2	16	6	4	6	15	8	5	2
Singing ...	400	59	173	134	316	41	111	132	491	65	156	233	787	81	234	399	452	37	136	241
Musicianship	—	—	—	—	56	19	14	13	118	28	41	41	89	12	24	46	160	33	52	57
Theory ...	942	126	—	674	1,023	294	—	667	2,364	479	—	1,610	17,388	—	—	15,217	5,231	—	—	4,956
	7,398	1,350	1,850	3,060	7,176	1,219	1,649	3,385	13,854	1,746	2,762	7,047	44,567	2,486	6,505	29,474	33,904	2,121	6,600	21,018
Piano Duets	32	8	18	6	58	12	29	15												
	Middle				*Junior*															

7 Singing Classes: 4 Distinction; 1 Merit; 2 Pass

2 Chamber music groups: 1 Distinction; 1 Merit

SUBJECT	Grade 3 Examined	Grade 3 Distinction	Grade 3 Merit	Grade 3 Pass	Grade 2 Examined	Grade 2 Distinction	Grade 2 Merit	Grade 2 Pass	Grade 1 Examined	Grade 1 Distinction	Grade 1 Merit	Grade 1 Pass	Total Examined	Total Distinction	Total Merit	Total Pass
Pianoforte...	20,917	1,405	4,839	12,381	23,294	2,023	6,220	13,151	26,411	3,127	7,455	14,101	110,994	9,409	26,708	61,369
Organ ...	4,816	482	1,282	2,632	6,039	550	1,540	3,356	7,637	642	1,907	4,378	623	161	257	176
Violin ...	340	41	97	180	398	37	107	229	1,329	226	429	612	26,473	2,812	6,905	14,117
Viola ...	1,251	199	432	552	1,280	226	427	555	—	—	—	—	1,752	260	492	854
Violoncello	131	13	29	70	—	—	—	—	—	—	—	—	6,523	1,207	2,116	2,793
Double Bass	862	40	214	494	—	—	—	—	—	—	—	—	388	44	121	179
Guitar ...	3,179	392	993	1,615	—	—	—	—	—	—	—	—	1,905	118	515	1,021
Flute ...	895	115	286	430	—	—	—	—	—	—	—	—	7,904	1,108	2,388	3,809
Oboe ...	6,191	439	1,572	3,648	—	—	—	—	—	—	—	—	2,913	484	999	1,252
Clarinet ...	197	52	72	66	—	—	—	—	—	—	—	—	14,792	1,077	3,625	8,524
Bassoon ...	890	77	240	496	—	—	—	—	—	—	—	—	711	163	252	262
Horn ...	2,389	145	580	1,405	—	—	—	—	—	—	—	—	2,044	237	556	1,057
Trumpet ...	928	86	243	505	—	—	—	—	—	—	—	—	5,378	399	1,340	2,984
Trombone	1,644	148	440	897	—	—	—	—	—	—	—	—	2,123	222	548	1,116
Other Brass	27	17	6	4	—	—	—	—	—	—	—	—	3,531	391	994	1,793
Harp ...	—	—	—	—	—	—	—	—	—	—	—	—	73	38	19	15
Singing ...	—	—	—	—	—	—	—	—	—	—	—	—	2,446	283	810	1,139
Musicianship	—	—	—	—	—	—	—	—	—	—	—	—	423	92	131	157
Theory ...	7,003	—	—	6,552	8,129	—	—	7,740	11,326	—	—	10,547	53,406	899	—	47,963
	51,660	3,651	11,325	31,927	39,140	2,836	8,294	25,031	46,703	3,995	9,791	29,638	244,402	19,404	48,776	150,580
Piano Duets													90	20	47	21
													244,492	19,424	48,823	150,601

24 Candidates were examined for LRSM: 16 in Dublin, 6 in Belfast and 2 in London;

1 in Branch B School Music, Sections II and III: (Fail);

2 in Branch D Performing: 1 Piano, 1 Flute (2 Pass);

30 LRSM General Papers (23 Pass, 7 Fail);

21 in Branch C Teaching: 10 Piano, 5 Violin, 1 Violoncello, 1 Flute, 1 Bassoon, 2 Trumpet, 1 Singing (12 Pass, 9 Fail).

Appendix C

Note on Kodaly, Orff, Suzuki and Rolland methods

Witnesses submitted reports on Hungarian music education in the primary school, based on methods formulated by Zoltan Kodaly. This approach involves Hungarian folk songs, hundreds of Kodaly compositions written for teaching purposes, relative solmization, handsigns and unaccompanied singing. In Hungary the approach has produced remarkable results in developing musicianship among school children. It is difficult to see a system so firmly-rooted in Hungarian culture and folk idiom transplanted into British schools, although attempts have been made to adapt it to a British context which some teachers are using. The Kodaly approach is also being used in schools in other countries, including the U.S., Canada and Australia. The real problem is that the Kodaly method requires teachers who are both excellent musicians (and these are by no means common in primary schools) and who have been specially trained in the appropriate teaching methods. It also assumes a continuity throughout the primary school, rarely found in music in British schools.

The so-called 'Orff method' has often been cited in evidence in connection with music in primary schools. The Carl Orff approach is concerned with the development of the whole child. It provides a framework in which children can respond creatively, through movement, dance and speech, as well as through instrumental music and song. In the systematic musical structure of the course, children start with limited notes, the pentatone, ostinato, small sequence and rondo forms through which they express themselves and improvise with notes and instrumental ensembles. It is true to say that the instruments introduced by Orff, particularly the xylophone, glockenspiels and metallophones, have now become part of the musical equipment of nearly every school in the country, and have made it possible for children with no skills on orchestral instruments, to take part in ensemble work. Although very few schools in the UK have adopted the Orff approach systematically, the philosophy and form of the methodology have become widely disseminated, like the instruments.

The Talent Education of Dr Shinichi Suzuki is a method by which thousands of Japanese children have learned to play the violin during their pre-school years. Dr Suzuki calls it the 'mother-tongue' method because he maintains the child learns the violin in the same way as he learns to speak. The mother *teaches* the child words by setting the example, by *repetition* at opportune moments. The baby *learns* the words and *sees* the mother saying them. The baby *imitates*, develops the *physical ability* to repeat the words, and has the *intelligence* to reproduce them. The baby will eventually *remember* the words and *understand* their meaning. Finally the baby experiences the emotional *meaning* of the words. The role of the mother is crucial in this learning approach. In Japan mothers receive about three months instruction on the violin before the child starts the instrument; but for the child to 'hear' good examples, records are used. Physical exercises have been developed by Dr Suzuki to aid co-ordination, and in the early years, the child plays from memory, using a 'marked' finger board, and only the upper half of the bow. An experiment recently carried out in this country indicates that the Suzuki method needs modifying to suit British conditions, particularly in its parental involvement, and its 'regimented' approach.

We should bring to the attention of string teachers the work of Dr Paul Rolland, who led the string research project at the University of Illinois. His ideas are being used at the ILEA Tower Hamlets music centre. In Dr Rolland's approach, there is an emphasis on purposeful musical 'games', and group activities to encourage complete relaxation and total body movement at the earliest stages. Music reading is approached through word rhythm memories, simple notation cards and using the voice.

Appendix D

Estimated number of full-time students taking music as a main[1] subject, by type of establishment, 1975

	GREAT BRITAIN	
	Number of *students*	*Number of* *establishments*
UNIVERSITIES		
Music departments with		
100 & over students	589	4
50 & under 100	656	10
under 50 students	483	18
TOTAL	1728	32
FURTHER EDUCATION COLLEGES		
Independent[2]	639	2
Direct grant[3]	1692	3
Grant aided[4]	1940	20
in establishments with		
200 & over music students[5]	3218	8
100 & under 200 ,, [6]	678	5
50 & under 100 ,,	164	2
under 50 ,,	211	10
TOTAL	4271	25
COLLEGES OF EDUCATION		
in establishments with		
100 & over music students[7]	262	2
50 & under 100 ,,	852	13
under 50 music students	2782	127
TOTAL	3903	142
TOTAL STUDENTS & ESTABLISHMENTS	9902	199

SOURCES AND NOTES

[1] Part-time students (at Further Education Colleges) numbered over 2000, of which half attended the Guildhall. About twenty establishments (not included in the figures in this table) provided only for part-time students.

[2] Guildhall School of Music and Drama, London College of Music.

[3] Royal Academy of Music, Royal College of Music, Trinity College of Music.

[4] Dartington College of Arts became grant aided in 1976 and is included under that heading.

[5] Guildhall School of Music, Huddersfield Polytechnic, London College of Music, Royal Academy of Music, Royal Northern College of Music, Trinity College of Music, Royal Scottish Academy of Music and Drama.

[6] Birmingham School of Music, Leeds College of Music, Colchester Institute of Higher Education, Welsh College of Music and Drama, Dartington College of Arts.

[7] Middlesex Polytechnic (Trent Park), Bretton Hall College.

SOURCE: Mainly DES, SED & UGC.

Appendix E

Number of persons in posts requiring a musical training, 1975
(Great Britain)

I. PERFORMERS (mainly full-time)[1]

   A. *Instrumentalists and Conductors*

Orchestras, chamber groups and soloists (including recording, T.V. and radio)	3,750*	
Theatres, dance halls, holiday camps, night clubs	1,400	
'Popular' music groups, including jazz, rock, 'pop', etc.	(3,000)	
B. *Singers*	1,000	9,150

II. TEACHERS

   A. *Schools – class teachers*[2]

Maintained schools			
Secondary – England & Wales[3]	13,250		
Scotland[4]	900		
Primary – England & Wales	(1,500)		17,000
Scotland	150		
Other schools	(1,200)		

   B. *Schools – peripatetic teachers*[2,5]   5,800

   C. *Further and Higher Education*

Universities[6]	201	
FE Colleges[7]	750	1,500
Colleges of Education[8]	550	

   D. *Private Teachers*   (2,300)

III. OTHER POSTS

A. Music Administration	(300)	(300)
B. Other	(100)	(100)

   TOTAL ALL POSTS   36,150

SOURCES AND NOTES

The Estimates are subject to wide margins of error. Not only are many musicians both performers and teachers but they may have a variety of part-time jobs (not necessarily in the music profession). The number of persons in the posts in the table relates mainly to those in full-time employment but, particularly in times of high unemployment, many musicians, particularly singers, may be working less than full-time. Moreover there is a wide range of employment, not included in the table, which by its nature is not full-time but for which a training in music is required. The income from this employment can play an important part in the life style of those musicians doing it and the musicians themselves make a significant contribution to the artistic life of the country. The type of activity includes, for example, cathedral church singers, church organists, as well as the very large numbers engaged on a casual basis in playing for dancing and clubs.

The figures in brackets have little factual basis and many others have been deduced indirectly from related sources.

[1] Sources of information are mainly the Musicians' Union, the Incorporated Society of Musicians and British Actors' Equity.

[2] Includes part-time teachers on a full-time equivalent basis: the number of persons teaching would be substantially higher.

[3] Teachers who spent on average half their time teaching music. (Source: DES).

[4] Teachers qualified to teach music. (Source: SED).

[5] Based on replies to a questionnaire from 15 LEAs representing 13 per cent of the school population.

[6] Source: UGC.

[7] Based on assumed teacher/pupil ratio of 1 to 6.

[8] Based on proportion of music to total students ($3\frac{1}{2}$ per cent) applied to total teaching staff at Colleges of Education (11,000).

* It is very difficult to give a precise breakdown of this figure because of the overlap between categories. Broadly, however, there were about 1000 conductors, soloists or performers in chamber groups, 1500 in contract orchestras and 1250 in other orchestras or free-lance players. Out of the total of 3750 over 1000 performers were mainly involved in recording, TV and radio.

Appendix F

Destinations of music students

I. DESTINATIONS OF MUSIC GRADUATES
AT UNIVERSITIES IN GREAT BRITAIN:
1975/76

		Percentages
Teacher training		34
Other training		14
Research and academic study		13
Employment		24
of which permanently employed in UK in		
Public Service	$3\frac{1}{2}$	
Education	4	
Industry and Commerce	2	
Publishing, cultural and entertainment organisations	4	
Other, including unemployed and unknown destinations		15
		100

II. DESTINATIONS OF A SAMPLE OF STUDENTS
LEAVING A LONDON MUSIC COLLEGE:
1973/74 & 1974/75

Teacher training		33
Other training, research and academic study		9
Employment:		
Music – Private teachers	5	
Orchestras	21	
Free-lance	9	
Soloists	$3\frac{1}{2}$	41
Opera	1	
Composition	$\frac{1}{2}$	
Administration etc.	1	
Other		10
Other, including unemployed and unknown destinations		7
		100

Appendix G

Universities in Great Britain with music courses (first degree) 1975/76

Aberdeen
Birmingham
Bristol
Cambridge
City
Durham
East Anglia
Edinburgh
Exeter
Glasgow
Hull
Keele
Lancaster
Leeds
Leicester
Liverpool
London
Manchester
Newcastle
Nottingham
Oxford
Reading
St Andrews
Salford
Sheffield
Southampton
Stirling
Surrey
Sussex
Wales
Warwick
York

Appendix H

Music students – estimated numbers of intending 'qualified' teachers

	1975			**1980's** *as implied in Report*		
		Outflow per annum[1]			Outflow per annum[2]	
	Total students	All Graduates	Intending[3] 'qualified' teachers	Total students	All Graduates	Intending[4] 'qualified' teachers
Universities	1728	600	200	2400	800	250
Music colleges:						
Trinity	374 ⎫			⎰ 400	100	100
Others	3897 ⎭ 1400		500	⎱ 3400	850	50
Other Higher Education	3903	1300	1300	1600	400	400
TOTAL	9902	3300	2000	7800	2100	800

[1] 3 year courses.

[2] Universities: 3 year courses; other institutions: 4 year courses.

[3] Our 'destinations' information suggests that one third of both university and music college students have been going on to take teacher training qualifications.

[4] Assumed proportions: universities – one third: music colleges (excluding Trinity) – 6 per cent.

NOTE

The DES say that, whereas, in the last 10 years the output of newly trained teachers was 30,000-40,000, the output in the 1980's is likely to be about 17,000 per annum and that, according to institutions' plans for 1981, an output of nearly 800 per annum is expected from all initial training courses for intending specialist music teachers in the 1980's (i.e., 4.7 per cent of the total). In 1975 we estimate that there were rather more than 20,000 such teachers in post compared with a total teaching force of about half a million (i.e., over 4 per cent).